3 Words That Spell

Investment Success

3 Words That Spell

Investment Success

The Truths
The Myths
The Madness

Charles W. Myers

3 Words That Spell

Investment Success

The Truths
> The Myths
> > The Madness

Charles W. Myers

I would like to thank Larry Wiggins for inspiring me to write this book and for all of his help and support.

Cover Photography: Martha L. Woods
Manuscript Readers: Marjorie Carlson-Hurst, Ph.D., Kevin Kroskey, MBA, Rev. Charles Erbe II
Editing: Larry Wiggins

To order this title or receive more information, please contact:

Chuck Myers
Charles W. Myers Investment Group / True Wealth Design
440 Layden Avenue
Canal Fulton, OH 44614
330-854-9701
www.truewealthdesign.com.

Dedicated to my family; wife - Marty, children - Sandie, Charlie, (Wendy) and John J., grandchildren - Kyle, Jordyn, Conner, London and Dominick, - 99-year-old mother, Celeste and to all other Alzheimer's patients.

Investment Success

The Alzheimer's Association
Before You Forget

Do you have a friend or family member who has been stricken with the terrible disease of Alzheimer's? If you do not already, you probably will. As many as 5.2 million people in the United States are living with Alzheimer's. One in six women and one in 10 men who live to be at least age 55 will develop Alzheimer's disease in their remaining lifetime. 10 million baby boomers will develop Alzheimer's in their lifetime. Every 71 seconds, someone develops Alzheimer's. On June 12, 2008, the Centers for Disease Control and Prevention reported that Alzheimer's disease is now the sixth-leading cause of death in the United States, surpassing diabetes. One of these statistics could be you or someone you love.

I became interested in Alzheimer's when I noticed that the disease affected many members of my clients' families. As I learned more about the disease I became more passionate in my resolve to make a difference. I have long said that anything I contributed to help fight this disease would be an investment in my own future. That prediction came true about two years ago when my then 97-year-old mother was diagnosed. She is still leading a happy life and just celebrated her 99th birthday. She helped to plan the surprise party.

The Alzheimer's Association is the only national non-profit organization dedicated to conquering Alzheimer's disease through research, and to providing education and support to people with the disease, their families and caregivers. Again this year, the Alzheimer's Association needs yours and my support.

Contact the Alzheimer's Association directly at www.alz.org for more information and to see how you can help or visit my website to support our Blue Chip team effort at http://cantonmemorywalk.kintera.org/cmyers

You might be helping yourself.

3 Words That Spell Investment Success

Contents

Introduction

Charles W. Myers brings to you more than 30 years of management, sales and client service experience. After graduating from St. Vincent High School in Akron (leading the way for LeBron James). Chuck went off to college where he majored in Fraternity. He was good at it. Later he returned to college with a different attitude. He graduated from Malone University with a Bachelor of Arts degree, a major in Business Management and a 3.9 GPA.

His financial credentials include Registered Representative (Series 7 License, currently inactive), Uniform Securities Agent (Series 63 License), Registered Investment Advisor (Series 66 License), and insurance licenses for Accident, Health, Life and Annuities. He operates his own firm the Charles W. Myers Investment Group and partners closely with the botique investmnt firm, True Wealth Design.

Chuck's clients include ages from those just starting out in investing to those already in retirement. He places special emphasis on seniors. He has often said that **"We are all seniors or aspire to be one."** This led Chuck to pursue his certification as a Certified Senior Advisor. **Certified Senior Advisor (CSA)**® is a designation earned through extensive training and by passing a comprehensive examination regarding the financial and social concerns facing seniors.

"Before people care what you know, they must know that you care."

Some of the ways Chuck and his wife Marty (Administrative Manager) serve the community are as officers of their local AARP Chapter. Both are members of the Canal Fulton Chamber of Commerce. Chuck is a member of the Canal Fulton Income Tax Review Board, Treasurer of the TAPS Committee for Canal Fulton, and Treasurer of the Canal Fulton Friends of the Library. Chuck also is Chairperson of the Northwest Stark Senior Citizens Center. He annually is put behind bars to raise money for MDA. In earlier years Chuck won the prestigious Jaycees Distinguished Service to the Community Award, helped teenagers in Junior Achievement and wore the big head dress as Nation Chief of Indian Guides.

Marty has attended the Barberton Church of God for over 50 years (only 37 years for Chuck). For the past 17 years she has been the Director of *Mother's Day Out*, the Christian Pre-School at the church. In addition, she also was a 17-year volunteer at Clinton Elementary School.

Both Chuck and Marty have a special place in their hearts for the Alzheimer's Association. They sponsor a team (Blue Chips) for the Alzheimer's Walk each year.

Chuck heads the Charles W. Myers Investment Group. He also is part of a small independent boutique Registered Investment Advisor (RIA) firm called *True Wealth Design*. They specialize in providing financial coaching to individual investors at all levels. As an independent firm they have the freedom to make decisions based on client needs and their own high set of morals without being dictated by upper management goals as found in corporate firms. A wise consultant once said, focus on what you do best and outsource the rest. Chuck's strength is in communications with and understanding clients, therefore this is his focus.

Chuck firmly believes in the Modern Portfolio Theory of investing. This theory strives to provide clients with market returns at low cost and through proper allocation of clients' portfolios. He believes his mission is to help clients live the one life they have in the best way they can, without undue financial sacrifice or overexposure to risk.

This book is a compilation of the thoughts, words and deeds of those who have come before Chuck and have impressed him as he has progressed through his career in the financial industry. The many myths that his clients had been bombarded with prompted him to write this book. The purpose of this book is solely limited to the dissemination of general information. Accordingly, Mr. Myers does not affect or attempt to affect transactions in securities, or the rendering of personalized investment advice or service for compensation through this publication. Although the information provided to you is obtained or compiled from sources we believe to be reliable, Mr. Myers cannot guarantee the accuracy, validity, timeliness, or completeness of any information or data made available for any particular purpose.

Chapter 1
Allocation, Allocation, Allocation.

The answer to investing is allocation, allocation, and allocation. How often do you get to start a book with the punch line? After you read this chapter you will not need to turn to the back of the book to see how the story ends.

This chapter will provide you with the basis of what you need to know to be a successful investor. The remainder of the book will demonstrate why this is true. Here we go.

There are many common misconceptions about investing that the average unsuspecting investor is bombarded with on a daily basis. Most of these misconceptions center around believing:

- Individuals and/or advisors can *consistently and predictably* provide superior skill in individual *stock selection*.
- Mutual Fund's *past performance* is a reliable way to predict which Mutual Funds or Mutual Fund Managers will have superior performance in the future.
- Professionals and individuals can effectively utilize *market timing* to predict when the market will go up and the market will go down.

We will investigate these myths in detail later in the book. For now, suffice it to say that **none** of these well-advertised methods of increasing the value of your portfolio have a very good track record. They just do not. What they do is sell readership or TV ratings

The method that does work has been identified and reiterated over and over. Still people do not listen or do not understand. It is said there are three words of importance in real estate. Those three are Location, Location and Location. In finding investment success there are also three words. They are Allocation, Allocation, and Allocation. These important words will work even if you put them in a different order. Let us try it! Allocation, Allocation, and Allocation. Let us try it once again in still a different order. Allocation, Allocation, and Allocation. See, it still works. Remember this!

In the simplest financial planning terms, there are three main asset classes. They are equities (stocks), fixed income (bonds and long-term CDs), and cash equivalents (cash, short-term CDs or Money Market). Each asset class has its positives and its negatives. You might remember these asset classes as your "Spend it money", your "Lend it money" and your "Own it money."

MAJOR ASSET CLASSES

	Spend it!	Lend it!	Own it!
Type:	Cash	Bonds	Stocks
Example:	CD < 1 yr.	CD> 1 yr.	Small
	Checking	Municipal	Mid
	Pass Book	Corporate	Large
	Mattress	Government	World
Return:	0% - 4%	4% - 8%	8% -12%
Positive:	Liquidity	Income	Hi Return
Negative:	Inflation	No Growth	Volatility

Figure 1

"Spend it money" is your cash and your investments that can be liquidated into cash in a short period of time, usually within a year. "Spend it money" normally brings a return of just over or just under the rate of inflation, currently in the range of 0% to 4%. This class's biggest advantage is liquidity. Money can be made available to you on short notice. The biggest disadvantage is that the investment may not keep up with the cost of inflation. Inflation is the biggest enemy to seniors on fixed incomes. If you are 20 years into retirement and inflation has averaged 2½% over that period, the purchasing power of your investment may be 50% of what it was when you retired, if your investments' rate of return hasn't kept pace.

I met a retired fellow that had his entire savings, $200,000, tied up in a no interest checking account. He received a pension and Social Security and did not need the money in his checking account to live on. I asked him what his intention is for that money. He said that in ten to 20 years, when he died, he wanted to pass it along to his children. Unfortunately, if he lives 20 years, inflation may reduce the purchasing power of the money left to his children by half. For him, I believe that his interests would be better served with asset allocation that reflected a little more aggressiveness, but not high risk.

Your "Lend it money" is the money that you lend to an entity for a longer term, a year or more. This asset class would include bonds, which are loans to a large entity such as a corporation or the U.S. Government. Bonds usually bring a return higher than cash, possibly 4% to 8%, depending on term and quality. People usually buy bonds for income. Typically they produce a steady income stream over the life of the bond. At the end of the bond's term, they return the principle. The disadvantage to this type of investment is that generally there is little or no growth. You receive only as much you put in.

Your "Own it money" is your piece of the rock. This is exemplified by ownership in the company itself in the form of stock. Buying stock allows you to own part of Coca Cola, Microsoft, Enron or other companies. Stocks traditionally produce the highest gains, 8% to 12% over time. Investors, who have faith in the growth of the economy and are looking for the largest return, purchase stocks. These investments are traditionally the most risky asset class among the three. The disadvantage to stocks is volatility. We have all seen wide short-term swings in the markets with values spiking at times and plummeting at other times.

In another instance, a newly retired friend of mine, who is a do-it-yourself investor, said he went from $1,000,000 in 2000 to $650,000 the next year. In 2004 he said that now he had excellent stocks and mutual funds. After looking at his portfolio I agreed with him that his choices were excellent. However, I asked him why he still had his investments in high-risk areas. He replied that these high risks were the only way he felt he could win his money back. Investing should not be gambling. Who knows when another investing year like 2000 will occur? For him, I believed that his financial goals would be realized with a more balanced, less aggressive allocation. If his allocation has remained the same, he took a tremendous hit again in the 2007 recession.

The above description of asset classes use the simplest terms for their definitions. Additionally, there are various sub-classes for these asset classes. When the sub-classes are employed in an overall asset allocation strategy, the portfolio's overall volatility is reduced and results are improved. We will explore these refinements later.

Asset Allocation is the process of selecting the correct mixture of asset classes for your individual circumstance. Studies have long confirmed that Asset Allocation represents virtually all of the probability of success in investing. However, some investors believe that picking stocks, hot fund managers, or timing when to get in or out of the market helps. Yet this is not what the academic studies show (Figure 2). While an investor using these methods may be lucky and out perform in the short run, in the longer term these factors are *negative* detractors from your investment return. If you are spending time on these other practices, it will be at the *expense* of your proper allocation and you will be rolling the dice with your life savings.

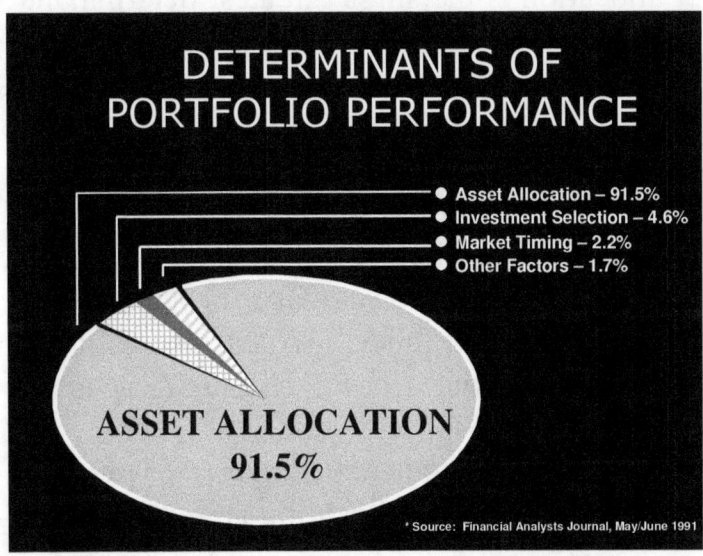

Figure 2

Investment Success

The study does not mean to say that stock selection and market timing can never add to performance. In aggregate, however, these activities hurt more than they helped, even when engaged in by very skilled investors.

If you miss identify your asset allocation, you can have the best selection of stocks, produced by the managers with the best track record for knowing when to get in or out of a market, you are still to likely fail.

Many people think their financial future is out of their hands because they can not control how world stock and bond markets do or how fast the U.S. economy grows.

While most people know the importance of regular investing, they frequently overlook the crucial role of asset allocation — allocation —spreading your investments among the asset classes and sub-classes.. As mentioned, studies have shown that asset allocation is the single greatest determinant of long-term investment performance. It can not be said enough that research has shown that 91.5% percent of the variation of returns on different portfolios may be accounted for by asset allocation.

Asset allocation "is the key decision that determines investment success, not how smart (or dumb) you are at picking stocks or mutual funds," writes Jane Bryant Quinn in *"Making the Most of Your Money"* (Simon & Schuster, 1997).

Asset allocation is all about not putting all your eggs in one basket. Simply stated, asset allocation is investing your money in different categories of assets — typically stocks, bonds and cash equivalents — so your investments are well diversified.

Asset allocation is based on the theory that the type or class of security you own is much more important than the particular security itself. It is a way to control risk in your portfolio. The risk is controlled because the asset classes in the well-balanced portfolio will react differently to changes in market conditions such as inflation, rising or falling interest rates, market sectors coming into or falling out of favor, recession, etc. If you put together two investments that tend to go in opposite directions in different market situations, the combination has a stabilizing effect on your portfolio. This is true even if individually the investments are both "risky," meaning they can and do deviate substantially from their expected returns.

How do you decide the correct asset allocation for your financial situation? The asset allocation process involves determining the proper blend of assets for your portfolio, one that will improve your chances of achieving your investment goals, while exposing you to a comfortable level of risk. No single investment plan fits everyone. You have to evaluate several factors before deciding on an asset allocation plan that fits your needs. Only after putting a strategy in place, should you begin individual security selection.

The main steps in an asset allocation strategy include:
1. **Identify** your life goals, defining them in measurable terms.
2. **Prioritize** your goals.
3. **Develop** a specific asset allocation strategy to reach your goals.
4. **Select** investments that fit your individual strategy.

5. **Monitor** and reviewing your progress through regular portfolio reviews.

HOW ASSET ALLOCATION HELPS INVESTORS MEET THEIR FINANCIAL GOALS.

Reduce Portfolio Risk — Asset allocation reduces the amount of volatility you experience by spreading market risk across many different asset classes (for example, value stocks vs. growth stocks). Different asset classes exhibit varying risk/return characteristics over periods of time. By spreading your portfolio among several asset classes with different behaviors, you may protect yourself from dramatic market swings.

Avoids Pitfalls of Market Timing and Stays Focused on Your Goals — A well-allocated portfolio alleviates the need to constantly adjust investment positions to chase market trends and helps reduce the urge to buy or sell in response to the market's short-term ups and downs. Keep in mind that while asset allocation cannot eliminate the risk of fluctuating prices and uncertain returns, it can help protect portfolios from severe market fluctuations and help you earn more consistent returns.

In developing your asset-allocation strategy remember that generally, the longer your investment time horizon, the more risk you can afford to take. Conversely as you get older and closer to retirement, you will probably be less interested in the growth of your portfolio and more interested in capital preservation, protecting the value of your portfolio from market declines by choosing less risky investments.

Investment Success

Determining your financial goals, a comfortable retirement, college education for the kids, purchase of a new home, probably is not too complicated, but developing a solid asset allocation plan designed to meet those goals may be. My experience reveals that determining the correct asset allocation and then sticking to it are the most difficult decisions that my clients face. A financial advisor is very helpful in this process.

Chapter 2
Are you a Stock Picker?

Return with me now to those thrilling days of yesteryear... the early 1980's. We wondered who shot JR and noted that nothing came between Brooke Shields and her Calvin Klein's.

We were also on the verge of a technological revolution. Many changes occurred during this time.

1980: Bill Gates licensed MS-DOS to IBM.

1981: IBM introduced the PC.

1982: Breakup of AT&T. Thank you Judge Green.

1983: Camcorders were introduced. Compact discs first released.

1984: The first megabit chip was made at Bell Labs.

1984: The term cyberspace was coined by William Gibson.

1984: Apple Computer released the Macintosh.

1985: Nintendo home entertainment system was introduced.

1986: Fox Network started in the United States.

1987: The largest stock-market drop in Wall Street

1988: CDs outsold vinyl for the first time ever.

1989: Time and Warner combined to become Time Warner Inc.

Investment Success

Imagine visiting your sick grandfather. Although you may have been just starting your career, he wanted to help you to look far ahead into your future and prepare you for retirement. He makes this offer to you. He will give you $1,000. With that $1,000 he asks that you select the best stock that you can think of and hold that single stock for 25 years.

You have narrowed your choice down to two companies; Motorola and Hormel, makers of SPAM. These are both excellent companies. Motorola is a leading electronics firm. SPAM became a staple in WWII and to this day is known as the state meat of Hawaii.

How many of us would have been able at that time to predict the technological revolution that was about to happen and would have had the insight to choose Motorola? The rest of us, I guess, would have chosen SPAM. Except perhaps if you went against your grandfather's wishes and put your $1,000 in a bank account with a safe 3% return.

For those with the insight of the technological revolution that was about to take place who chose Motorola, you did quite well. In the 25 year period between 1980 and 2005 Motorola's value increased by 1,569%. That is almost $1.6 million. Good job! For those who chose Hormel, you did OK too. The makers of SPAM, Hormel, saw its value increase by a whopping 5,947%. I could retire rather comfortably on $5.9 million.

I point this out to demonstraste to you how difficult it is to choose that one or two stocks out of all that are available that will hit a home run. To do it consistantly is even harder. You often hear from stock pickers and gamblers about the times they won. You seldom hear them brag about the times they lost.

Oh by the way, if you had put your $1,000 in something seen as safe at 3%, your value would have grown to less than $3,000.

I agree with whoever said, "We have long felt that the only value of stock forecasters is to make fortune tellers look good."

Chapter 3
Are the Pros any Better?

Have you seen the articles in the Wall Street Journal that pit people throwing darts at a wall full of available stocks against professional investment managers? More often than the professionals would like to admit, the dart throwers get higher returns on their mixes than the professionals do. This poses the question, "If these money managers and the Wall Street Journal cannot beat a simple toss of a dart, then how do money managers perform as a whole and specifically, how does this apply to mutual fund managers?"

Morningstar, using Principia Software data through 12/31/07, conducted a study to determine how mutual fund managers compared to a simple broad index like large US stocks. In this case they used the S&P 500, which is just a collection of the largest 500 stocks in America.

The study determined that only about 30% of the money managers performed better, or beat the market, at least **half** of the time and 70% of the mutual fund managers consistently performed worse than the S&P 500. That percentage is dismal.

This number could actually be worse but mutual fund companies are becoming more and more adept at merging poor performing funds into other funds that happen to be doing well. This phenomenon is known as survivorship bias and it is nowhere to be found in the prospectus. Survivorship bias is one of the many reasons that stock pickers' returns look better than they actually are. You find survivorship bias when mutual fund managers tout their fund's performance based on comparisons with an average mutual fund. This average is calculated from a list of funds that have survived during a particular period. Funds that did not survive the period are not included in the calculation. Another study by Vanguard showed similar results.

We are considering that these experts are supposed to be the brightest and the most insightful people in the world as far as picking stocks. If they are, this is not particularly impressive. In fact, I do not believe the active professional manager is any better at picking stocks than you or I.

So if only 30% of the money managers seemed to do better, or beat the market at least **half** of the time, why don't we just follow their funds and buy them? Not so easy, as we shall see.

Why not just pick the best and most successful managers? Should we follow the advice of the 30% of the money managers that beat the marked half of the time? These

Investment Success

managers seemingly are the best and have the best track record of results.

According to Morningstar Principia, January 1998, top performing funds in the ten-year period between 1988 and 1997 were:

1. Fidelity Sel Home Finance
2. Kaufmann
3. Hancock Regional Bank B
4. Fidelity Sel Regional Banks
5. Invesco Financial Svcs
6. Chase Vista Growth & Inc A
7. Fidelity Sel Electronics
8. Seligman Communicate & Info A
9. Pilgrim Bank & Thrift A
10. Fidelity Sel Health Care
11. Vanguard Health Care
12. Fidelity Contrafund
13. T. Rowe Price Science & Tech
14. Fidelity Adv Eqty Grth Instl
15. Fidelity Sel Brokerage & Invmt
16. Skyline Special Equities
17. Invesco Technology
18. FPA Capital
19. Fidelity Sel Medical Delivry
20. Fidelity Sel Financial Svcs

Let us suppose that you are sitting down with your broker in January of 1998. What funds do you think he or she would be recommending? I think there is a very good chance of them recommending funds that were on this top 20 list for the past ten years. What do you think?

Investment Success

Now let us go back and revisit the top 20 funds, ten years later, at the end of 2007. If you do this, you will see that not one of these funds repeated on the list. **Not one.** If we could determine which funds to buy by picking successful managers, should not a number of the funds repeated over the next ten years?

We may discover at least a part of the answer to this question by looking at one of the best stock pickers of all time, Peter Lynch of the Magellan Fund. Some would say he was a genius at picking stocks. Others would say he was just lucky. For now, let us assume that he was a genius. Peter Lynch took the reins in May 1977 and remained the manager of Magellan for thirteen years. During this time period, the fund averaged a 29% annual return. You would think that one with his analytical qualities would be well suited to choose a good manager as his successor. If you look at the performance of the Magellan Fund since he left the reign, you would not think so. The fund has not come close to Lynch's level of success since his departure.

Professor Mark Carhart at the University of Chicago studied the mutual funds that existed between 1961 and 1993 and found that on average, actively managed funds under-performed their index by about 1.80% per year. Similar findings are outlined in the groundbreaking paper entitled *Returns from Investing in Equity Mutual Funds 1971 to 1991* by Burton Malkiel, the Princeton professor who authored *A Random Walk Down Wall Street.*

According to Vanguard, for the ten years prior to 2007, the majority of actively managed U.S. stock funds underperformed compared to the index they sought to outperform. For instance, 84% of actively managed U.S. large blend funds underperformed their index, and 68% of actively managed U.S. small value funds underperformed, as well. The situation is even worse for actively managed bond funds. Almost 95% of actively managed bond funds underperformed their indexes for the same time period.

For the period of December 31, 1992 to December 31, 2007, only 41.6% of actively managed U.S. large company funds that beat the S&P 500 in a particular year were able to exceed the S&P 500 in the next year. After three years, only 9.7% of the original group still performed better than the index. The performance is similar for actively managed small cap funds and emerging market funds.

Bottom line. Mutual Fund Managers are poor stock pickers and there is no correlation between a manger's ability to pick stocks and their ability to continue to perform at the same level in the future.

Chapter 4
Market Timing

When should I cut my losses and get out of the market? When should I get back in? These are both good questions. These questions both refer to a strategy of timing the market. The answers to these important questions are not found in the markets themselves. Market timing does not work. The reason to change your portfolio is that your life situation has changed and not because of market dropped or gained.

If you have a very aggressive portfolio allocation of stocks and the market falls, on paper, you will lose accordingly. If you are allocated properly, however, and do not need to touch that money for a number of years, then you are in perfect position to benefit from the subsequent upswing. Conversely, if you have a very conservative portfolio, mainly in fixed assets, and the market takes off, it is not the time to move into stocks. In either case, if you are allocated correctly, you should be patient and let the markets work for you. If on the other hand, you are not properly allocated or if changes in your life cause your allocation strategy to change, this is the perfect time to consider reallocation.

An oft-quoted DALBAR, Inc., *Quantitative Analysis of Investor Behavior, 2007* study, shows that the average investor earns significantly less than the market indices, and investors that time the market actually **lost** money over the period measured. In fact, during the 20-year period between 1987 and 2006, the S&P 500 index rose 11.8% while the average investor gained only 4.3%. For market timers, the results were even worse. This group lost 1.8% over the study period. Their latest study shows even worse results. For 20 years ended December 31, 2008 the S&P 500 advanced 8.35% while the average investor made just 1.87% each year. "The reality is that investors are not rational and make buy and sell decisions at the worst possible times." So says Louis Harvey, Dalbar president. A motto for these irrational investors could be, "When the going gets tough, investors panic."

During the 1987 - 2006 study, the average investor's holding time was only three years rather than the 20 years that the study encompassed. Rather than buying a fund and holding it for the long-term, the average investor chased market performance. Sometimes they did this upon the advice of their broker, by buying funds that had a good track history. Others moved to the hot fund or the hot sector of the day. They did not follow an allocation strategy; instead they overloaded an asset class because the current result was better. They believed that either they or their advisor had a crystal ball to guide their judgments. This method usually is not fruitful. Have I mentioned **Allocation, Allocation and Allocation?**

Chapter 5
The Bulls and Bears

While there are conflicting views of what constitutes a Bull Market and what constitutes a Bear Market, one thing seems true. Bull Markets usually last longer than Bear Markets. This fact alone puts timing the market at a disadvantage. A Bull Market is when the market is going up, like a bull thrusting his horns upward upon attack. A Bear Market is when the market is going down, like a bear swiping down with his claws as he attacks.

From January 11, 1973 until December 6, 1974, one of our most severe Bear Markets, the Dow Jones Average dropped – 45%. What would have happened if you had tried to time the market during that period? The period started by a six month drop of 38% in Large Cap Stocks. Would this have told you to get out of the market? Five months later it dropped another 20%, followed in another two months after with a 19% increase. If you retreated from stocks, that increase might be

---

the signal to you to reenter market. However, three months later, a nine-month period followed with the Dow down another 46%.

Surely by this time you are convinced that the market is doomed and is no place for you. Oops, just the next month the Dow surged back 37% and in the succeeding six months gained an astounding 71%. This increase was followed by three months of slight losses and then the market surged again, gaining 42% over the next six months. Small Cap Stocks reacted similarly over that period of time. Similar patterns occurred during the tech crash of 2000 and even during the Great Depression.

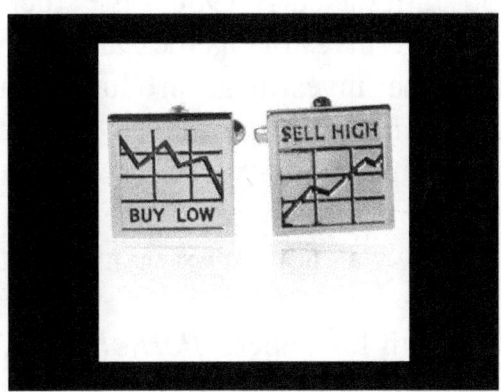

What we would like to do: Buy Low – Sell High

Many investors who try to time the market end up selling low and buying high, which is exactly the opposite of what they intend to do. It is better to be patient, recognizing that short-term market changes are easier to detect than long-term trends. As we have discussed earlier and as the studies suggest, market timing does not work!

Chapter 6
Basis of Beliefs – Why I believe what I believe

So far, we have investigated what does not work. Before I start building a portfolio that does work, I would like to point out why I believe as I do. My beliefs do not come from the TV and Press pundits selling their wares. The basis for my beliefs comes from analyzing the progression of the financial industry over the past eighty-five years. They come from academia's finest, many Nobel Laureates, who have added credence to what is known today as Modern Portfolio Theory.

From about 1935 until the early 1950's the stock markets were not as open to average investors as they are today. Information on investing and the investment products was not readily available. It was assumed that if an investor were to take a risk in the market, he would need a very large return. By choosing a single company, he had a better chance of hitting that home run. Diversity usually was not a major consideration.

Harry Markowitz with his paper *"Portfolio Selection,"* which appeared in the 1952 *Journal of Finance*, introduced the concepts of what later came to be known as the Modern Portfolio Theory. The Modern Portfolio Theory (MPT) demonstrates how investors can use diversification to optimize their portfolios, thus reducing risk. The basic concepts of the theory are diversification, the Efficient Frontier and the Capital Asset Pricing Model (CAPM). Markowitz won the Nobel Prize in Economics for his work.

Investment Success

Markowitz begins with the assumption that all investors prefer to avoid risk, whenever possible. He defines risk as a standard deviation of expected returns. You may also think of this as volatility. Rather than look at risk on an individual security level, Markowitz proposed that you measure the risk of an entire portfolio. When considering a security for your portfolio, do not base your decision on the amount of risk that it carries. Instead, consider how that security contributes to the overall risk of your portfolio.

Markowitz then considers how all the investments in a portfolio can be expected to move together in price under the same circumstances. This is called correlation and it measures how much you can expect different securities or asset classes to change in price relative to each other. For example, even in a market downturn there are some items, such as grocery staples, that every household still needs. Therefore, a stock in this category and a tech stock might do better in this market than two high growth tech stocks. When you put all this together, it is possible to build a portfolio that has a much higher average return than the level of risk it contains. Building a diversified portfolio and spreading your investments by asset class, manages both risk and return.

For most investors, the risk when they buy a stock is that the return will be lower than expected. In other words, does the return on the investment deviate from the average return? Each stock has its own standard deviation from the mean, which Modern Portfolio Theory (MPT) calls "risk". The risk in a portfolio of diverse individual stocks will be less than the risk inherent in holding any single individual stocks (provided the risks of the various stocks are not directly related).

Consider a portfolio that holds two risky stocks: one that pays off when it rains and another that pays off when it doesn't rain. A portfolio that contains both assets will always pay off, regardless of whether it rains or shines. Adding one risky asset to another can reduce the overall risk of an all-weather portfolio. In other words, Markowitz showed that investment is not just about picking stocks, but about choosing the right combination of stocks to minimize risk in one's portfolio.

If you are going to invest your hard-earned money, you naturally want to minimize your risks, while maximizing your potential returns. MPT suggests that you can limit the volatility in your portfolio, while improving its performance, by spreading the risk among different types of securities that do not always behave the same.

It is a principle of investing that the higher the risk, the higher the potential return and conversely, the lower the risk, the lower the return. According to MPT, a portfolio exhibits risk and return characteristics based on its composition and the way those components correlate with each other. For every level of return, there is one portfolio that offers the lowest possible risk, and for every level of risk, there is a portfolio that offers the highest return. These combinations can be plotted on a graph. This meeting point of each level of risk and reward, where the optimal portfolios reside, is called the "Efficient Frontier"(Figure 3). An efficient frontier is a set of portfolios that each maximizes expected return for a given level of risk.

Your goal should be to maximize your return for the amount of risk that you are comfortable accepting. To do that, you need a properly allocated and diversified portfolio.

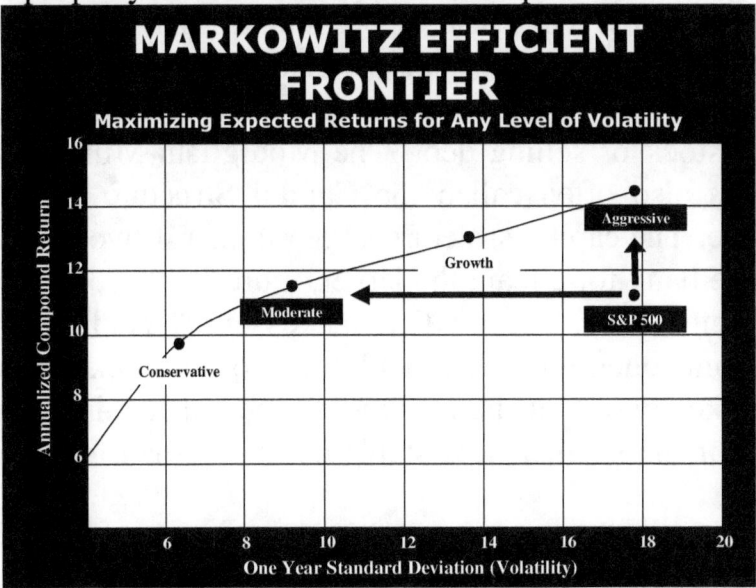

Figure 3   **Efficient Frontier of Optimal Portfolios**

William Sharpe, also a Nobel Laureate, further demonstrated this principle as in his Capital Asset Pricing Model (CAPM), created for risk-adjusted investment performance analysis. The CAPM is a model for pricing an individual security or a portfolio. The market reward-to-risk ratio is effectively the market risk premium. In layman's terms, we know how much return can be expected in a very safe United States Treasury Bill. By gauging the risk and return of other securities or portfolios against this base, we develop a standard deviation. The theoretical model defines risk as volatility relative to market. Using this model we can evaluate risk and reward of an individual security or even in an entire portfolio. The higher the reward to risk ratio, the more volatile the security or portfolio.

Investment Success

In 1961, Merton Miller & Franco Modgliani, also Nobel Laureates in Economics, published a theorem about corporate finance stating that a company's value is unrelated to its dividend policy. The basic theorem states that in an efficient market the value of a company is unaffected by how that firm is financed. It does not matter if the firm's capital is raised by issuing stock or selling debt. The Modigliani-Miller theorem (MM) is also often called the Capital Structure Irrelevance Principle. The capital structure suggests that if two companies go to the bank for a loan, the larger, more stable company will get a better rate. Doesn't that make sense? Additionally, if these companies go to the public and offer stock, doesn't it also make sense that the stockholder would require a greater return for the smaller, less stable company than for the large one?

Another financial milestone occurred in 1965 when the A. G. Becker Corporation started the financial consulting industry with the creation of their "Green Book" performance tables comparing results to benchmarks. These are the first studies showing that investment professionals fail to outperform market indexes, as quoted by Michael Jensen, in *"The Performance of Mutual Funds in the period 1945-1964," Journal of Finance," December 1965.*.

Paul Samuelson of MIT, who also won a Nobel Prize in Economics, determined that market prices are the best estimates of value, price changes follow random patterns, and future stock prices are unpredictable. He is famous for saying "Investing should be dull, like watching paint dry or grass grow. If you want excitement, take $800 and go to Las Vegas. It is not easy to get rich in Las Vegas, at Churchill Downs, or at the local Merrill Lynch office." It would follow that this demonstrates that we are not very good at picking stocks.

In 1965 Eugene F. Fama came on the scene. Fama set out to develop a comprehensive theory to explain why stock market prices fluctuate randomly. He coined the famous phrase *"Efficient Market."* In January 1965, the Journal of Business published Fama's entire Ph.D. thesis, *The Behavior of Stock Market Prices*, which also was summarized by the *Financial Analysts Journal* and titled *"Random Walks in Stock Market Prices."*

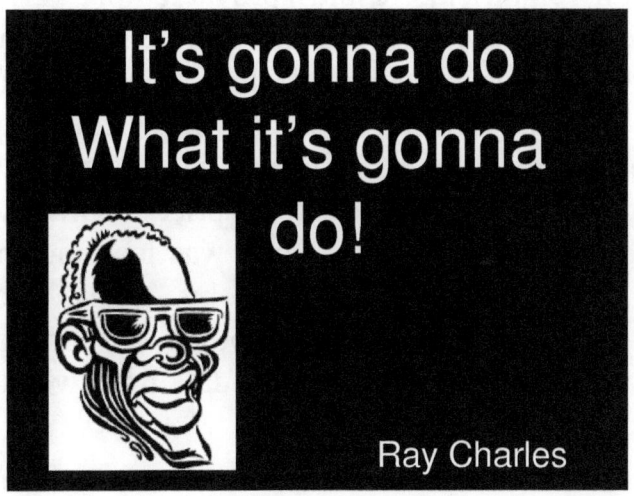

The Efficient Market Theory is an investment theory that states that it is impossible to "beat the market" because stock market efficiency causes existing share prices to always incorporate and reflect all relevant information. As Ray Charles says, "It's gonna do what it's gonna do!" Information about stocks is widely and cheaply available to all investors. According to the Efficient Market Theory, this means that stocks always trade at their fair value on stock exchanges, making it impossible for investors to either purchase undervalued stocks or sell stocks for inflated prices. Stock prices will almost instantaneously change as new unpredicted information about them appears in the market. As such, it should be impossible to outperform the overall market through expert stock selection or market timing and the only way an investor can possibly obtain higher returns is by purchasing riskier investments. All of these factors make it almost impossible to capture returns in excess of market returns, without taking greater than market levels of risk.

This is an empirical result, provable or verifiable by experience or experiment. Based on time-series analyses of past prices, Fama concluded that prices behaved like geometric random walks. This theory threw cold water on the practice of technical analysis, suggesting the predictive price patterns technicians derived from price charts were only figments of their imagination. Fama was learning for himself what is widely accepted today by many professional investors—that data mining can produce all sorts of trading systems that work beautifully on the data from which they are derived but are worthless otherwise.

Studies on this subject go back to 1932 when Alfred Cowles studied the performance of investment managers and investment newsletters. Presumably, the recommendations from these sources employed a variety of analytic techniques to make their stock picks. Their collective poor performance cast doubt, not only on technical analysis, but also on all means of speculative trading. In short, the vast majority of mutual funds lag the market. They do this not because their managers are stupid but because beating the market is

Investment Success

extremely difficult. Fund buyers who want to give themselves the best chance of success should therefore choose among low-cost passive funds.

A.G. Becker Company gave us a benchmark or index with their "Green Book" in 1965. We could not however, buy the entire index at that time. Along came John McQuown, at Wells Fargo Bank in 1971 and Rex Sinquefield, at American National Bank in 1973. With them came the birth of the index fund. It was a few years later that a major company committed to invest in an index. In 1975 New York Telephone Company invested $40 million in an S&P 500 Index fund. This event helped launch the era of indexed investing that we see today.

In 1977 Roger Ibbotson and Rex Sinquefield performed extensive database studies of securities prices, collecting extensive public market information dating back to 1926. At the time, this was the most comprehensive empirical studies of stock market returns and became one of the most widely used databases. You may have found some of Roger Ibbotson's charts on the walls of investment offices. They are sometimes referred to as Ibbotson Charts, Growth Charts or Mountain Charts. Using this information we can calculate the risks and rewards of different asset classes over different periods of time. We'll put this in practice later.

In 1981, a University of Chicago Ph.D. named Rolf Banz published *"The Relationship between Return and Market Value of Common Stocks"* in the *Journal of Financial Economics*. The conclusion was startling: Between 1931 and 1974, small-company stocks had thrashed the market's giants. This new evidence dovetailed beautifully with the Modern

Portfolio Theory. MPT argued that risk was linked with return. Since small-cap stocks unquestionably carried higher risks than large-cap stocks, it would only be logical for them to deliver higher returns.

Allocation, Allocation, Allocation. The Financial Analysts Journal, May/June 1991 in *"Determinants of Portfolio Performance"* by Brinson, Singer and Beebower showed that Asset Allocation is 91.5% responsible in determining a portfolio's performance. The remaining responsibility consists of asset selection (4.6%) market timing (2.2%), and other factors (1.7%). **91.5% is big, take note!**

Let us revisit William Sharpe's use of his Capital Asset Pricing Model (CAPM) for a moment. In 1992 Eugene Fama and Kenneth French from the University of Chicago, and Dartmouth College respectively, introduced their Multifactor Asset Pricing Model and Value Effect in *"The Cross Section of Expected Stock Returns,"* published in the *Journal of Finance,* June 1992. Their research improved on the Sharpe's single-factor asset-pricing model. CAPM identified market, size and value factors affecting returns. Their development of the three-factor asset-pricing model is an invaluable asset allocation and portfolio analysis tool and revolutionizes the way investors and advisors construct and analyze portfolios.

All of the concepts discussed in this section can be used to improve portfolios. Some of the enhancements over time to these concepts have led to the construction of portfolios based on asset class rather than just indexing. This practice captures specific dimensions of risk identified by financial science rather than allowing commercial index benchmarks to dictate a strategy. High transaction costs and turnover is part and parcel of indexing. On the other hand, asset class construction of portfolios minimizes transaction costs and enhances returns through portfolio design and trading, since the portfolios are not slaves to benchmarking.

The advantages to asset class investing are so conclusive that today, over $1 TRILLION of institutional money is passively invested in asset classes. Only 20 years ago, that number was about $50 million. Most individual investors don't know about asset class investing because the financial press and brokerage houses do not sell magazines or earn commissions by showing you its benefits.

Some companies, most notably Dimensional Fund Advisors (DFA), have improved on the model even further by constructing core equity strategies. Each core strategy targets the entire stock market as its eligible universe. But unlike traditional approaches, the securities are not held in their market value proportions. The portfolios increase the relative weight of small cap and value stocks, where expected returns are greater. Because the architecture is seamlessly integrated and includes the full range of securities, the costs normally associated with maintaining multiple vehicles are greatly reduced. They are designed to capitalize on opportunities presented by broad economic factors, opening new and flexible solutions to everyday investment challenges.

Dimensional Fund Advisor's Vice President James Davis reviewed the academic research on equity mutual-fund performance from 1969 to 2001 and summarized it this way.

With some minor exceptions, the research shows the following:

- The vast majority of actively managed funds lag passive benchmarks.
- Some fund managers do have above-average stock-picking skill, but usually not enough to allow them to overcome the costs of their own trading and compensation.
- Almost all fund performance can be explained by four "factors": the market's performance, the relative size of the stocks in the portfolio, the relative valuation of stocks in the portfolio, and the relative "momentum" of stocks in the portfolio. These factors have little to do with traditional "stock-picking."
- The market is not perfectly efficient, but its inefficiencies are not large or regular enough to exploit consistently.

These theories presented by Nobel Laureates and academia's finest form the basis of my beliefs. From these theories, I have embraced the following guiding principles:

- Market prices already reflect all known information.
- Risk factors determine the expected rate of return.
- Diversification reduces the risk of uncertainty.
- Asset allocation principally determines results in the portfolio.
- Time in the market is more important than market timing.

Chapter 7
Letters of the Law

The first two acronyms that I would like to examine are RR, Registered Representative, and RIA, Registered Investment Advisor. Either of these agents can use various titles and many investors do not know that there is a difference between them. Be aware that Financial Analyst, Financial Adviser (Advisor), Financial Consultant, Financial Planner, Investment Consultant or Wealth Manager are generic terms or job titles, and may be used by investment professionals who may not hold any specific designation. I have been both a Registered Representative (RR) and Registered Investment Advisor (RIA). I recognize that there is a substantial difference between these positions. I started my financial career as a Registered Representative for a large brokerage firm. Everyone has to start somewhere.

I was not there very long when I discovered that I did not like their business model. I was registered with the NASD, now called FINRA and had a Series 7 license. We were commissioned salespeople. I was not a fiduciary, meaning I was not legally obligated to act in my client's best interest. I made money on commissions or fees from what I sold. I sold products that may, or may not, meet my clients' needs. I offered advice to meet their needs, but this was legally incidental to my job. I became aware of articles that suggested that the market is moving away from this type of compensation, especially for more affluent clients. I could understand why.

Registered Representative (stockbroker)

- **Brokerage firm primarily in the business of buying and selling securities**

- **Registered Representative typically an employee/contractor of brokerage firm**

- **Typically compensated by commissions on product transactions**

- **Held to suitability standards, not fiduciary standards**

- **Often "look like" an advisor in marketing collateral and Web sites**

- **Regulated primarily by FINRA (but also by SEC and states)**

Figure 4

I also noted the requirements for me to progress in the brokerage business. Since I was generally paid up front on commission, if I added a new client one month, I would either have to sell them something new or find another new client the next month. Over time, this would cause me to have many more clients than I could personally provide service. After leaving this structure, I was told by a new client that his former Registered Representative (RR) had bragged with glee that when he opened his new account that he was his 8,000th customer. Even having five percent of this many clients would make it impossible for me to provide personal service.

The strucure of the business had made me concerned about the appearance of a conflict of interest. If I were paid on what product I sold, would it seem to the client that I was making my recommendation based on what was good for him or for what paid me the most commission? I worked with many RRs who were professionals that I believed to be moral and upright and I suspect they kept the customer's need in mind. I didn't believe that the structure of the Registered Representative (RR) supported this. The stucture of this business model itself didn't incent me to be client focused and made me feel very uncomfortable.

I had worked for large companies most of my career. These large companies always said that what was good for the customer was good for them. Sometimes though they seemed to act in a way that was beneficial to them, even if it were at the expense of the customer. At any brokerage firm that I worked I was never actually forced to sell what the company recommended. Our traning did however lean largly toward favored providers and we were incented to use them. At other companies, I was told, some departments, such as underwriting or banking, would pressure the sales force to promote products because they were highly profitable, when they were known to be inferior. Some were fined substantially for practices such as these.

Investment Success

All of these points led me to a conclusion. That is that a Registered Representative (RR) is for practical purposes a point of sale relationship. That means that you can go to them and buy investments. They will sell them to you or you can tell them what you want. Sometimes they will be great at their position and treat you like they were a Registered Investment Advisors (RIA). Sometimes they will treat you like they are an RIA and then not follow through and act with your best interests in mind. As I mentioned before, for the RR this wasn't a requirement but rather legally just incidental to the job.

I discovered that there was a different way. The Registered Investment Advisor (RIA) is a different story. They are not allowed to charge commissions and your fee agreement is in writing. They have to act in your best interests by law at all times. So your worry about conflicts of interests is lessened.

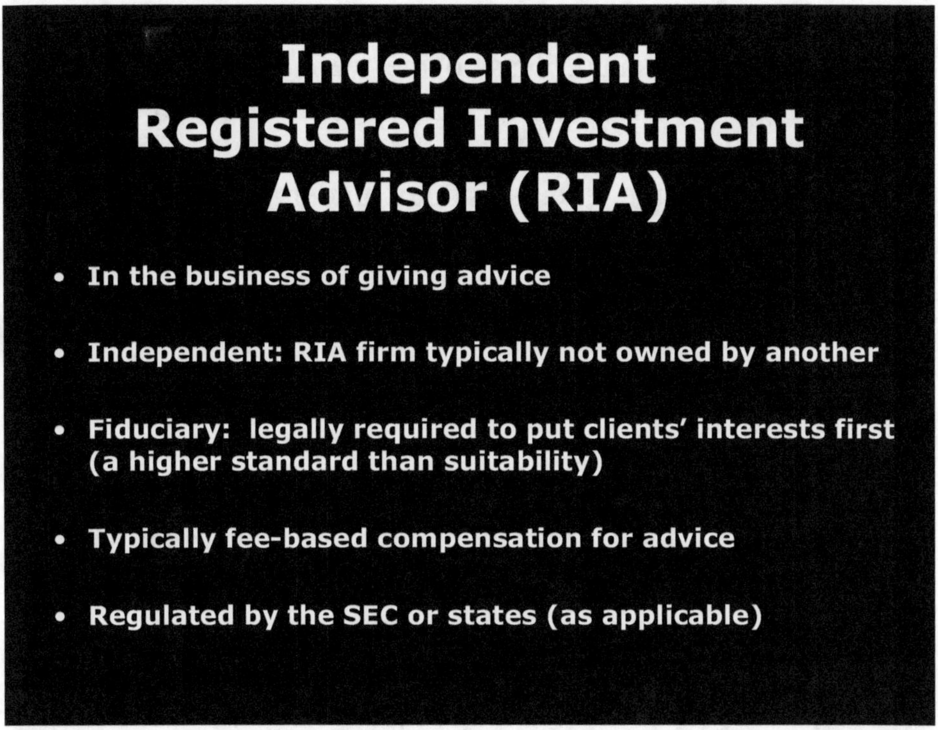

Investment Success

Figure 5

I determined that the RIA is in the best position to give each client the peace of mind that they deserve. No conflicts of interests because of commissions exist. The RIA truly puts the client and the Advisor on the same team. They are also required by law to serve the client's best interests. I do not think that all Advisors are good just because of the law and there are still RIA's out there that are not good at what they do. I do believe that their structure at least makes them more accountable. Registered Investment Advisors (RIA) are required to hold a Series 65 or 66 License and be registered as an Investment Adviser with the SEC or their local state. They are legally required to act as fiduciaries, meaning they are legally obligated to act in your best interest. They provide big picture financial planning and money management. They are fee based compensated. This to me went a long way toward eliminating the inherent conflict that existed with a commisioned salesperson. Under a fee system, I would charge a percentage of the clients money under management. The funds or securites that I used made no difference as far as my compensation. Lastly, since I would be paid on an ongoing basis, I would be financially incented to provide excellent client service. If I do not, clients would leave me and I would have a reducion in my income.

As an RIA you manage a client's mutual fund portfolio. You likely would no longer put clients in those funds that RRs use with chokingly high fees, 12b-1 fees, high turnover and enough inefficiency to make a knowledgeable investor cringe. A 12b-1 fee is one that is charged by some mutual funds (usually actively managed funds), which is used to pay marketing, distribution, and service costs, and is paid to the broker. The Financial Industry Regulation Authority (FINRA) allows funds to charge as much as 1.00% annually as a 12b-1 fee. Rather, you would buy clients low load institutional funds from Dimensional Fund Advisors, Vanguard, Fidelity or Exchange Traded Funds (ETF) and others. These funds do not have 12b-1 fees, the turnover is very low, and you do not have the usual style drift found in many of the funds sold by RRs. There also is as much as a 2% or more annual advantage over the funds sold by RRs. As an RIA you charge your ongoing fee to manage the portfolio. The client saves money, they get better products and they get more of my attention.

My background has been in business solution selling. That meant that in order to serve a client you had to understand their business and come up with a solution that fit their needs. When I moved to the financial industry my attitude didn't change. When I moved to the RIA fee based structure I was financially incented to continue in this vein.

The general public is quite confused as to the terms and functions of the Registered Representative (RR) and Registered Investment Advisor (RIA). In 2004 and 2006, TD AMERITRADE commissioned a survey of over 1,000 United States Investors. 74% were not aware that only RIAs have a fiduciary responsibility to act in investors' best interests. This means the adviser must hold the client's interest above his own in all matters. 58% of investors believed both stockbrokers and Independent Registered Investment Advisors have a responsibility to act in their best interest. 63% believed that stockbrokers and Independent Registered Investment Advisors were both required to disclose all conflicts of interest before providing financial advice. 81% were concerned that both stockbrokers and investment advisors provide fee-based advice, but offer different levels of protection. 89% said they would rather work with an investment advisor if they knew advisors provided greater investor protection than stockbrokers.

Only our government could add to this confusion with official titles. Wouldn't one think that if you passed the Series 65 or 66 exam that your title would be a Registered Investment Advisor (RIA)? Well no. The firm is the RIA. The person who passed the exam and who runs the firm or is employed by the firm is called an Investment Advisory Representative (IAR). I am sure that clears things up.

To add more confusion, now some Brokerage Firms can actually now offer some fee-based advice. If they do, a disclosure such as this is required in the fine print on the bottom for a Brokerage Firm:

THIS IS A BROKERAGE SERVICE
The Securities and Exchange Commission requires all broker-dealers who give brokerage advice for a fee to make the following disclosure. Accounts enrolled in this service are brokerage accounts and not advisory accounts. Our interests may not always be the same as yours. Please ask us questions to make sure you understand your rights and our obligations to you, including the extent of our obligations to disclose conflicts of interest and to act in your best interest. We are paid both by you and, sometimes, by people who compensate us based on what you buy. Therefore, our profits, and our salespersons' compensation, may vary by product and over time. Please call us at XXX-XXX-XXXX if you have questions about the differences between a brokerage service and an advisory service.

After reading the disclosures on a brokerage firm's Web site, 79% of investors said that they would be less likely to go to a brokerage firm for financial advice.

To add another level of confusion, you can be a Registered Representative (RR) a Registered Investment Advisor (RIA) and even an insurance agent, all at the same time. I think this is fine as long as you are acting in the best interest of the client. More and more, however, I see presentations given by Registered Investment Advisor (RIA) firms that seem to be nothing more than pitches for high commissioned annuities.

There is considerable confusion in the investment community regarding financial advice and the people who dispense it. Do not be confused. Check them out.

Chapter 8
More letters

I am a college graduate with a Bachelor of Arts (BA) degree majoring in Business Management and am a Certified Senior Advisor (CSA®). That by itself doesn't mean than I am smarter than anyone else who may not have these same credentials. I do think that the designations infer a few things. One thing is that I made the effort. Secondly, I think that it gives some insight into what I hold out as being important. The BA might indicate that I was interested in a more broad education than perhaps a more specialized area such as Electrical Engineering would provide. The major in Business Management might indicate that I am interested in how companies are run. The **CSA®** might indicate that my interests lie with seniors.

I believe the same to be true of the many letters after a name. The Financial Industry Regulatory Authority (FINRA) lists about 50 letters or designations in their database. While FINRA does not approve or endorse any professional designation it does list them so you can see for yourself.

FINRA is the largest non-governmental regulator for all securities firms doing business in the United States. All told, FINRA oversees nearly 5,000 brokerage firms, about 172,000 branch offices and approximately 663,000 registered securities representatives. Created in July 2007 through the consolidation of NASD and the member regulation, enforcement and arbitration functions of the New York Stock Exchange, FINRA is dedicated to investor protection and market integrity through effective and efficient regulation and complementary compliance and technology-based services.

FINRA touches virtually every aspect of the securities business—from registering and educating industry participants to examining securities firms; writing rules; enforcing those rules and the federal securities laws; informing and educating the investing public; providing trade reporting and other industry utilities; and administering the largest dispute resolution forum for investors and registered firms. It also performs market regulation under contract for The NASDAQ Stock Market, the American Stock Exchange, the International Securities Exchange and the Chicago Climate Exchange.

I believe that examining some of the letters or acronyms of designations found on the FINRA website may give you some insight into your representative, just as looking at the letters of a college degree gives some insight as to the collegiate. Looking at FINRA's site (www.finra.org) you will find their listing of designations.

The first one listed is **Accredited Asset Management Specialist (AAMS)**. The AAMS website (www.cffp.edu/portal/alias) states "The growing emphasis on building lasting client relationships and gathering assets under management is changing the way the investment community conducts business." This is accomplished in 11 modules taking about 96 to 120 hours to complete.

Might you infer from that designation that the owner is interested in building lasting relationships and increasing their assets under management? On FINRA's website, however, it shows that an AAMS designation requires no prerequisites, no educational requirements, and no continuing education or experience. It lists no process for investor complaints or public disciplinary. It also shows no way to check an AAMS's professional's status online and shows no accreditation.

Let us compare this to another one on the site that you may have heard of; Certified Financial Planner (CFP®). The College for Financial Planning was originally founded to formalize financial planning, set high standards, and establish a rigorous certification process for financial services professionals. In 1972, the College for Financial Planning introduced the Certified Financial Planner™

certification. CFP® certification has evolved into the world's most recognized and respected financial planning credential, with more than 50,000 professionals in the United States having earned the designation.

CFP® follows a rigorous educational course. Candidates must have a bachelor's degree (or higher) from an accredited college or university, and 3 years of full-time personal financial planning experience. Candidates must complete a CFP® board registered program, or hold a CPA®, ChFC®. Chartered Life Underwriter (CLU®), or CFA® designation. They may also qualify by holding a Ph.D. in business or economics, be a Doctor of Business Administration, or have an Attorney's License. They have a continuing education requirement of 30 hours every two years. There is an online complaint and disciplinary process and you can check a CFP's status online. This last note is very interesting. The Certified Financial Planner (CFP) along with the Certified Senior Advisor (CSA®) are the only ones listed on the FINRA website that show an accreditation agency.

The Society of Senior Advisors (SCSA®) educates professionals to work more effectively with their senior clients. They believe that the right kind of planning, recommendations and referrals can make aging a state to be savored instead of a fate to be feared. For those who work with seniors, that means understanding the key health, social and financial factors that are important to seniors—and how these factors work together. **Certified Senior Advisors (CSA$^®$) have** supplemented their individual professional licenses, credentials and education with knowledge about aging and working with seniors.

One might infer from a Certified Senior Advisor (CSA$^®$) designation that the professional is interested in understanding and helping seniors. As I have said, "We are all seniors or aspire to be one." The FINRA website notes no prerequisites to be a Certified Senior Advisor (CSA$^®$) and a three and a half day live classroom requirement. They must, however, complete 18 SCSA credits every three years. As with the CFP$^®$, there is an online complaint and disciplinary process and you can check a Certified Senior Advisor's (CSA$^®$) status online at www.society-csa.com. And along with the Certified Financial Planner (CFP$^®$) they are accredited by the National Commission for Certifying Agencies (NCCA).

Licenses, credentials and education alone do not certify expertise in financial, health, social matters, or any other field, but I do think it shows where your professional's interest lie and that they at least made the effort.

Chapter 9
Annuities

I am not much of a proponent of annuities. I think they have their place but are a niche product. They also have a very high compensation value for the person who sells them.

I believe that this high compensation, sometimes as high as 10% and more, causes them to be grossly oversold to the public instead of used only when and where appropriate in a client's portfolio. If I were to fill a new $400,000 client's portfolio with annuities, it wouldn't be unusual for me to make $30,000 to $40,000 in commissions. Since the client is paying that commission whether they realize it or not, I think that many clients would be better served in a proper allocation of stocks and fixed assets at rates that are much lower.

Let us start out with a definition of annuities from the Securities and Exchange Commission. An annuity is a contract between you and an insurance company, under which you make a lump-sum payment or series of payments. In return, the insurer agrees to make periodic payments to you beginning immediately or at some future date. Annuities typically offer tax-deferred growth of earnings and may include a death benefit that will pay your beneficiary a guaranteed minimum amount, such as your total purchase payments.

There are generally two types of annuities—Fixed (FA) and Variable (VA). A third type, Equity-Indexed Annuity (EIA) has some features of both the FA and the VA.

In a Fixed Annuity (FA), the insurance company guarantees that you will earn a minimum rate of interest during the time that your account is growing. The insurance company also guarantees that the periodic payments will be a guaranteed amount per dollar in your account. These periodic payments may last for a definite period, such as 20 years, or an indefinite period, such as your lifetime or the lifetime of you and your spouse. Fixed Annuities are not securities and are not regulated by the SEC.

Fixed Annuities (FA) are essentially CD-like investments issued by insurance companies. Like CDs, they pay guaranteed rates of interest, in many cases higher than bank CDs. I see Fixed Annuities (FA) as being designed for seniors over the age of 70, primarily for the wealth preservation and transfer of their cash asset directly to their beneficiaries or to provide a guaranteed lifetime income stream. The convenience and predictability of a set payout makes a Fixed Annuity (FA) a popular option for retirees who want a known income stream to supplement their other retirement income.

They are not designed for someone to put their money in and take it right back out like some day trader playing the Stock Market like a flea market swap meet. They still have many of the same downsides as other forms of annuities. Those include tying up your money for an extended period of time, surrender charges, and high commission rates for person who sells them. As an Asset Class, I see them falling between the Cash and Bond Class. They tie your money up as do bonds but generally offer you less return.

Investment Success

In a Variable Annuity (VA), by contrast, you can choose to invest your purchase payments from among a range of different investment options, typically mutual funds. The rate of return on your purchase payments, and the amount of the periodic payments you will eventually receive, will vary depending on the performance of the investment options you have selected.

Variable Annuities (VA) are notorious for the fees they charge. The average annual expense on variable annuity subaccounts currently stands at 2.44% of assets, according to Morningstar. (This figure includes fund expenses plus insurance expenses.) The average open-ended mutual fund (excluding municipals), on the other hand, charges 1.32%, which I still think is extremely high compared to indexes, ETFs and asset allocated funds. Unfortunately, Variable Annuity (VA) fees do not stop there. Many Variable Annuities (VA) act like 'B" shares of mutual funds, paying commission from the ongoing fees. They also have an average contract fee of $30 to $35.

I see Variable Annuities (VA) as lying between Bonds and Stocks on the Asset Class Chart. They offer you less return than stocks in a normal mutual fund. Another problem with most variable and other annuities is that your money is often locked up for several years. Variable Annuities (VA) are securities regulated by the SEC.

Who might consider a Variable Annuity (VA)? If you are in the 25% tax bracket or higher; and you have have maxed out your other tax-advantaged retirement accounts, such as your 401(k) and IRA, and you do not tend to be a buy-and-hold investor of tax-efficient mutual funds, and are at least 15 years from retirement, then maybe a Variable Annuity (VA) fits into your plan. But those are a lot of "ifs."

You can learn more about Variable Annuities (VA) by reading the Securities and Exchange Commission's publication, *Variable Annuities: What You Should Know.*

An Equity-Indexed Annuity (EIA) is a special type of annuity. During the accumulation period – when you make either a lump sum payment or a series of payments – the insurance company credits you with a return that is based on changes in an equity index, such as the S&P 500 Composite Stock Price Index. The insurance company typically guarantees a minimum return. Guaranteed minimum return rates vary. After the accumulation period, the insurance company will make periodic payments to you under the terms of your contract, unless you choose to receive your contract value in a lump sum.

Equity-Indexed Annuities (EIA) combine features of traditional insurance products (guaranteed minimum return) and traditional securities (return linked to equity markets). Depending on the mix of features, an Equity-Indexed Annuity (EIA) may or may not be a security. The typical Equity-Indexed Annuity (EIA) is not registered with the SEC.

Equity-Indexed Annuities (EIA) have been somewhat controversial. For one thing, they come in more different versions and different formulas than Carter has pills. I do not know how many pills Carter has but my mother used to say that. That makes each company's policies difficult to compare. With all the different scenarios it is under what conditions which version will do better than others. I believe that they also give investors the impression they'll be getting more upside than they probably do and those selling them many times overemphasize the value of the downside protection. For most, if capital preservation is important to you, I think Equity-Indexed Annuities (EIA) and other annuities are an expensive way to get principal protection, in large part because of the big commissions many of them provide to the people who sell them.

According to FINRA, the guaranteed minimum return for an EIA is typically 90% of the premium paid at a 3% annual interest rate. However, if you surrender your EIA early, you may have to pay a significant surrender charge and possibly a 10% tax penalty that will reduce or eliminate any return.

You can learn more about Equity Indexed Annuities (EIA) by reading the SEC's online brochure, which explains them and provides resources for obtaining additional information. This information can be found on the SEC's webpage: www.sec.gov/answers/annuity.htm.).

Are Equity Indexed Annuities (EIA) good for anyone? Let us say that you are planning to retire immediately or within a few years and that you want to begin turning some of your retirement savings into a stream of cash that will support you in retirement. In that case, an annuity can be a good choice because annuities have one feature no other investment has, they can generate a lifetime income. You invest a certain amount of money in the annuity, and the insurer pays you income that can last the rest of your life no matter how long you live. In this case, you are not using the annuity for tax shelter as much as a retirement income vehicle. I believe that in most cases, however, a client is better off with a well-allocated portfolio of mutual funds.

Most annuities provide a death benefit. The death benefit basically guarantees that your account will hold a certain value should you die before the annuity payments begin. With basic accounts, this typically means that your beneficiary will at least receive the total amount invested — even if the account has lost money. For an added fee, this figure can be periodically "stepped-up" or earn a small amount of interest. (If you opt not to annuitize, then the death benefit typically expires at a certain age, often around 75 years old.). Given the fact that stocks have returned an average of 12% annually (assuming dividends are reinvested) from 1926 to 2007, according to the Center for Research in Security Prices, over the long haul you need this insurance about as much as a cow needs wings. Smart Money adds that Variable Annuities (VA) are sold more aggressively than fake Gucci handbags on the streets of New York City.

As with most retirement accounts, if you withdraw funds before age 59 1/2, you'll be hit with a 10% early withdrawal tax penalty. A payment from an annuity is considered ordinary income, and will be taxed at your marginal rate (also known as your tax bracket). For many of us, that is 25% to 35%. Compare that to the tax treatment of other investment income. Due to recent tax-law changes, dividends and long-term capital gains will be taxed at a maximum of 15%. And that tax difference can easily eat up the advantage of an annuity's tax-free compounding. "You are generally going to have to wait 15 to 20 years before these suckers become more tax efficient than a mutual fund," says CFP Dee Lee of Harvard, Massachusetts.

Most annuities impose "surrender charges" that penalize policyholders who pull out of the annuity within a specified number of years. Typically, the penalty is 7% if the policy is cancelled within the first year, 6% the second year, 5% the third, and so on until the surrender charge vanishes. The average maximum fee is a steep 5.94%, according to Morningstar.

There's no getting around the income tax due on annuities. In fact, if you die with money remaining in your annuity, your beneficiary will inherit all the taxes that you have deferred. Compare this to a mutual fund, whose basis is stepped-up at death. In that case, your beneficiary would owe no taxes on the gains. Both types of accounts — annuities and mutual funds — are liable for federal estate taxes on anything over the federal estate tax exemption.

The truth is that annuities only make sense for a tiny fraction of the population. The rest of us should be buying plain old mutual funds. Of course, that's not easy to say to your dark-suited cousin who keeps taking you out for steak and high priced wine in hopes that you will sign on the dotted line. For those lucky investors who bought annuities and then died within the next two months, their families probably got their money's worth. But, consider this: The death benefit was triggered in only 1% of all policies from 2002 to 2004, according to Limra International, an insurance-industry research group.

I believe that there is more of a place in a client's portfolio for choosing a Fixed (FA) or an Equity Indexed Annuity (EIA)than there is for a VA. EIAs too have many of the same drawbacks as do variable annuities but they are, at least, more than just mutual funds packaged within an insurance policy as are variable annuities.

Many times annuities are sold by those inviting you and possibly your spouse to a free dinner and presentation. Sometimes their real motives are hidden in the wording. They do not need everybody who attends to buy. A few in the audience buying may cover all of their costs and provide them with a substantial income. Think twice before accepting their next invitation.

Chapter 10
Defining Risk

We do not need Tom Cruise to tell us that just living is a very risky business. Driving to work, crossing the street, or even just lounging in our backyard hammock all involve some degree of risk. Imagine the risk my wife took when she answered yes to my marriage proposal many years ago. We take prudent steps to manage those risks, mostly without even thinking about them. We use our car's seat belts. We make sure no vehicles are approaching before crossing the street. We strap ourselves in when we go zip-lining (but we go zip-lining). And we do not hang the hammock too far above the ground. Investing, of course, also involves risk. But you can manage those risks and still sleep at night if you understand the different types of investment risks and how they can affect your portfolio. Many times when a Financial Advisor talks about risk he or she is talking about volatility, but overall risk is the uncertainty tied to any investment decision. Since few of us can accurately predict the future, risk is always a factor in the decision-making process.

Like the Tooth Fairy and Peter Pan, risk free investments are a fantasy. When it comes to investing, risk and reward are inextricably entwined. All investments involve some degree of risk. If you intend to purchases securities, such as stocks, bonds, or mutual funds, it is important that you understand before you invest that you could lose some or all of your money. The reward for taking on risk is the potential for a greater investment return. If you have a financial goal with a long time horizon, you are likely to make more money by carefully investing in asset categories with greater risk, like stocks or bonds, rather than restricting your investments to assets with less risk, like cash. On the other hand, investing solely in cash investments may be appropriate for short-term financial goals.

Roger Ibbotson ends his book *Path to Investing* in this way. "You may have heard the phrase, 'the only constant is change itself. Nothing could be more true about the world of investing. In fact, the only constant in the financial markets is that their values will go up at some point just as surely as they will go down. Your first line of defense in dealing with this uncertainty is knowledge. Safety is achieved by understanding all of the risks of an investment, not just the obvious ones."

Financial risk comes in many forms. Here are some:

Asset-backed securities risk - Asset-backed securities are debt securities backed by pools of assets like mortgages, auto loans, and leases. Payments of principal and interest from the loans backing these securities are passed through to the investors in these securities. The values of these securities vary with changes in interest rates. Asset-backed securities that are not backed by mortgages have additional risks. For example, some of these loans may be unsecured, meaning that there is no collateral for the loan. If the issuer defaults, there is no collateral to collect to cover losses. State and federal consumer credit laws that may be very favorable to borrowers at the expense of investors also may protect borrowers. Asset-backed securities can be more difficult to value or trade if a regular trading market does not exist for these securities.

Banking industry risk - Banks may be particularly sensitive to certain economic factors such as interest rate changes, adverse developments in the real estate market, fiscal and monetary policy, and general economic cycles.

Bond Risk - While bonds are considered less risky than stocks, rising interest rates may produce periods of negative total returns for the bond portion of your portfolio. Also, structuring a portfolio that is well-diversified among stocks, bonds, and money market investments will also reduce your overall portfolio risk. The market value of bonds typically goes down when interest rates go up. Longer-term bonds are generally more sensitive to interest rate changes, meaning they may suffer deeper declines in value than shorter-term bonds.

Credit risk - If the financial health of a security issuer declines, the price of its debt securities could decline or become more volatile, or the issuer could default on its securities (fail to pay interest or principal when due). High-yield securities have more credit risk than investment-grade securities.

Currency risk - The risk of fluctuating exchange rates. For example, it is possible the investment itself (say in Japan) provides a positive return of 10% but because the Yen loses 10% of its value relative to your currency the return to you is 0%.

Economic Risk concerns the strength or weakness of near-term economic growth and its impact on investment return.

Foreign risk — bond investments - Any investment in a foreign issuer will have the risks of political and economic instability, poor regulation, insufficient issuer information, controls on currency, high taxes or tariffs, and the confiscation of assets. These risks may be greater in emerging or developing markets.

Foreign risk — emerging markets - Securities markets of developing countries involve greater risks than those of more developed markets. Securities markets in developing countries are generally smaller, less liquid, more volatile, and more subject to manipulation than U.S. markets. Developing countries may have significant economic liabilities, such as inadequate infrastructures, obsolete financial systems, excessive regulation, significant international debt, volatile inflation rates, and environmental problems. Their economies may be heavily dependent on a limited number of export commodities, and their agriculture may be highly vulnerable to climate patterns. Developing countries also have higher risk of political instability, popular unrest, and armed conflict.

Foreign risk — money market investments - U.S. dollar-denominated securities from foreign issuers can pose greater risks than those from U.S. issuers, for reasons that include less stringent regulation, accounting, and reporting practices, as well as the higher risk of political, financial, and economic events among other factors.

Foreign risk — stock investments - Investments in foreign stocks may be more volatile than investments in U.S. stocks and may perform differently from the U.S. market. Foreign governments might change stock exchange rules, increase taxes or confiscate investors' assets. The governments of foreign countries might be less stable than the U.S. government, and issuers in foreign jurisdictions might have less thorough regulation and accounting, auditing and recordkeeping requirements. It might cost more to invest directly in a foreign stock than it would to invest in a U.S. stock. Changes in foreign currency exchange rates could also affect the value in U.S. dollars of foreign securities.

Fraud risk - The risk of losing investments due to fraud, for example the company doctoring their books or an investment adviser taking assets. Some of these risks are partially covered by government insurance in the USA but only in certain situations and to certain limits.

High-yield bond risk - High-yield bonds, also known as junk bonds, are rated below investment grade because there are doubts about whether the companies or entities that issue them will be able to pay interest and principal back on time. Junk bonds pay out higher interest rates than investment grade bonds because they present higher risk and are considered speculative.

Income risk - The rate of income that a fund or underlying fund generates may go up and down as interest rates go up and down. The amount of any dividends you receive will fluctuate over time.

Indexing risk - By using an indexing strategy, a mutual fund forgoes the option of taking any steps to lessen the impact of market downturns. In addition, a mutual fund that uses an index strategy might not perform as well as the index it aims to match ("tracking risk"). The existence of mutual fund fees and expenses, which an index itself does not include, make this risk very likely.

Illiquidity Risk is the possible absence of a buyer (or market) in the event that you are forced to sell. This typically affects real estate and collectibles.

Inflation Risk is the possible erosion of your purchasing power. An investment must yield a rate of return that exceeds the current rate of inflation to be considered profitable. If you invest most or all of your money in so-called "safe" investments like money
market funds, you will barely stay ahead of the rising cost of living. Over long periods, inflation can wear away at your purchasing power. The antidote to inflation risk is to invest at least some of your money in growth. Many times I advise even retirees to invest at least a portion of their portfolio in stock investments, depending on their individual risk tolerance. Over time, low-risk income investments may fail to keep pace with inflation, making them potentially a poor choice for long-term investing.

Interest-rate risk occurs when the direction of leading interest rates changes, directly affecting the value of an investment. Rising interest rates usually accompany periods of rising inflation. While higher rates may boost the yield on your fixed- rate investments such as money market investments, inflation reduces your real rate of return (your actual rate of return minus inflation). Higher interest rates usually are a negative for stocks and for bonds. Higher interest rates mean higher costs for many businesses, adversely affecting their bottom lines and, in most cases, their stock price. The price of a bond or bond fund moves in the opposite direction of market interest rates.

Interest rate risk — money market investments - During periods of rising interest rates, money market fund yields may tend to be lower than prevailing market rates.

Investment grade securities risk - While all securities rated at least Baa (by Moody's) or BBB (by Standard & Poor's) are considered investment-grade, ratings are only the opinions of the companies issuing them and are not guarantees as to quality or an assurance of performance or quality of such investment.

Liquidity risk - A fund or underlying fund may be unable to pay redemption proceeds within the time period stated in this prospectus because of unusual market conditions, an unusually high volume of redemption requests, or other reasons.

Manager risk - The investment adviser of a fund or underlying fund may make investment decisions that fail to produce the intended result. These may include decisions about how to allocate assets among different underlying funds, when to rebalance a fund, when to change underlying fund allocations, or which securities to buy and sell and when.

Market risk is the possibility that the value of an investment will either depreciate or appreciate because of fluctuations in the financial markets. This is the type of investment risk you may think of first. It is the risk that the overall market will fall, bringing down your stocks or funds along with it. The market values of stocks, bonds, and other securities may go up and down as securities markets react to economic, political, geographic, or regulatory factors. These factors may affect the entire market or just certain securities, industry segments, or economic sectors. In general, stock prices have fluctuated more than bond prices over longer time periods. Price changes may be temporary or may last for extended periods. The best way to manage market risk is not by trying to time market swings, a strategy that almost always fails in the long run, but by steadily investing in a diversified mix of investment types.

Money market fund risk - Although a money market fund seeks to preserve the value of your investment at $1.00 per share, it may not succeed in doing so and you might lose money by investing in a money market fund.

Political Risk is the possibility that domestic or global political events may affect the stability of return on an investment.

Real estate investment trust risk The value of a REIT can be hurt by economic downturns or by changes in real estate values, rents, property taxes, interest rates, tax treatment, regulations, or the legal structure of the REIT. Any stock issued by a REIT is also subject to stock market risk

Rebalancing risk A fund may temporarily stray from its target mix among the underlying funds and not perform as well as if it had invested according to its target mix at all times.

Reinvestment risks - The risk that future proceeds will have to be reinvested at a lower potential interest rate. Because market prices for certain debt securities (such as mortgage backed securities, asset-backed securities, and callable bonds) are based on expectations of how interest rates will behave, any unexpected behavior of interest rates can hurt performance for owners of these securities. For example, a drop in interest rates may mean a security is paid off earlier than expected, and the proceeds can only be reinvested at a lower rate. A rise in interest rates can mean that securities are paid off later than expected, leaving investors locked into below-market rates.

Small company risk The stocks of smaller, less well-known companies are generally more volatile than large company stocks and may perform differently from the market as a whole. Compared to larger companies, small companies may be poorly understood by investors, have less access to cash and credit, and may be heavily dependent on a limited number of products, services, or technologies.

U.S. government securities risk Although the U.S. Treasury guarantees securities issued directly by the U.S. government, securities issued by an agency or instrumentality of the U.S. government may not be. No assurance can be given that the

U.S. government would provide financial support to its agencies and instrumentalities if not required to do so by law.

Variable and floating rate securities risk Variable rate securities readjust their interest floating rate securities readjust their interest rates whenever a particular interest rate changes. Interest rates on these securities are normally tied to, and are a percentage of, a widely recognized interest rate, such as the yield on 90-day U.S. Treasury bills or the prime rate of a bank. These securities have interest rate and credit risk. They also may have liquidity risk because it is not always easy to sell these instruments if the issuer defaults or a fund or underlying fund cannot exercise "demand" rights. Demand rights, which are normally a feature of these investments, allow an investor to demand that the issuer repay immediately all unpaid interest and return the principal, the original investment amount.

Chapter 11
Reduction of Risk Over Time

It is crucial to develop an investment mix that is suited to the level of risk you are willing to assume. The point where you stand on the risk/reward spectrum depends on variables like age, family situation, current and expected future income, tax bracket, and overall net worth. Investment objectives are best met by a blend of assets that match your risk tolerance, specific lifestyle, and long-term needs.

Asset Allocation (have I mentioned allocation before?) is an approach in which you invest in different asset categories — mainly cash, fixed income, and equities. By diversifying your money across and within these asset classes, you can help minimize risk and potentially improve your overall returns. Therefore, by diversifying your investments over several asset classes, you may actually reduce your risk and volatility while achieving strong returns. The asset allocation that works best for you at any given point in your life will depend largely on your time horizon and your ability to tolerate risk. It sounds simple, and it is. But it is not easy.

An investor with a longer time horizon may feel more comfortable taking on a riskier, or more volatile, investment because he or she can wait out slow economic cycles and the inevitable ups and downs of our markets. By contrast, an investor saving up for a retirement that is just a few years away would likely take on less risk because he or she has a shorter time horizon.

Risk tolerance is your ability and willingness to lose some or all of your original investment in exchange for greater potential returns. An aggressive investor, or one with a high-risk tolerance, is more likely to risk losing money in order to get better results. A conservative investor, or one with a low-risk tolerance, tends to favor investments that will preserve his or her original investment.

If we look at the S&P 500 Index's range of returns for various time horizons since 1926 we see some wide levels of volatility, or risk. An investment matching the performance of the Index held for a one-year period ranged from a 163% gain from July 1932 to June 1933 to a 68% loss from July 1931 to June 1932. That is significant volatility. However, holding the same investment for twenty years returned as much as 18% per year from April 1981 to March 2000 and never less than 1% from September 1930 to August 1949. It is important for investors to remember the market may fluctuate in the short-run, but returns tend to stabilize in the long run.

Investment Success

Over the long term, periods of high returns tend to offset periods of low returns. With the passage of time, these offsetting periods result in the dispersion of returns gravitating or converging toward the average. In other words, while returns may fluctuate widely from year to year, holding the asset for longer periods of time results in apparent decreased volatility.

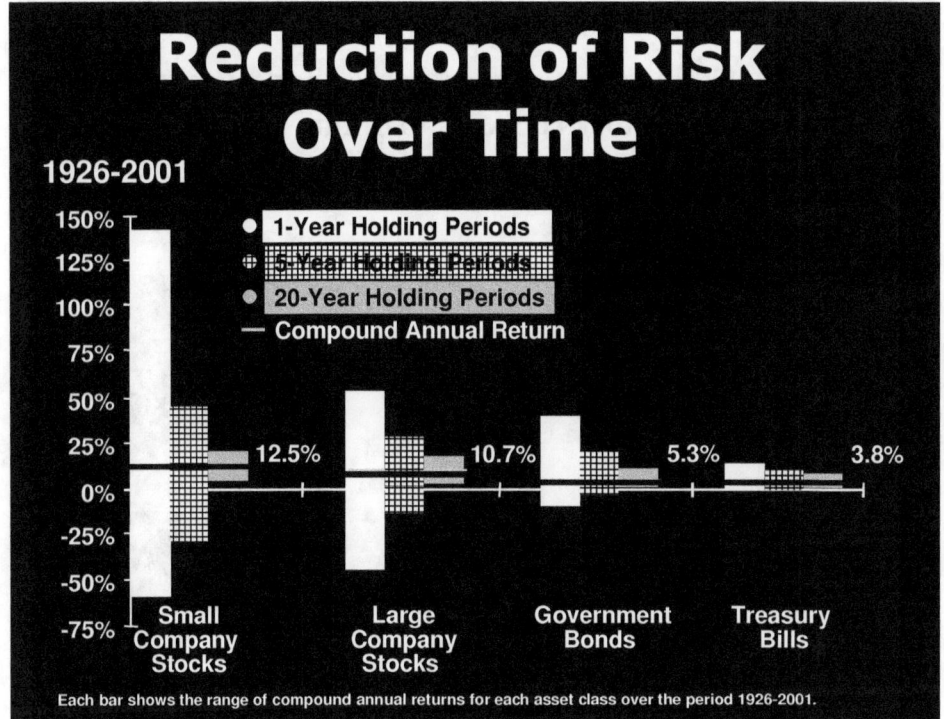

Figure   **6**

In Figure 6 you can see, using the information brought to us by Roger Ibbotson, we can calculate the risks and rewards of different asset classes over different periods of time. This graph illustrates the range of compound annual returns for stocks, bonds, and cash over 1, 5, and 20-year holding periods. On an annual basis since 1926, the returns of large company stocks, for instance, have ranged from a high of 54% to a low of –43%. For longer holding periods of five or 20 years, however, the picture changes. The average returns range from 29% to –12% over five-year periods, and between 18% and 3% over 20-year periods. The good news is that during the worst 20-year holding period for stocks since 1926, stocks still posted a positive 20-year compound annual return.

Although stockholders can expect more short-term volatility, the risk of holding stocks appears to diminish with time. To properly align your risk/reward formula you must find your proper allocation.

Chapter 12
Learning from the Laureates – If we build it.

We have seen what the scholars have said. Now let us see what we can learn from them. Remember the acadameans conclusions that the market prices goods and services appropriately and that prices are random and unpredictable. Further, since all knowable information is already in the current price, it is unlikely for someone to consistently find undervalued or overpriced securities. What this tells us is that it is not possible for anyone to consistently predict where prices will go. The randomness of the market makes it impossible for any individual or entity to consistently predict market movements and capture additional returns unrelated to risk. Therefore it is prudent to build portfolios that capture the returns of all markets including all global markets.

Harry Markowitz Nobel Laureate taught us that diversity with low correlation and proper allocation are the keys to investment success. His Capital Asset Pricing Model (CAPM), originally developed in 1952 was fine-tuned by William Sharpe another Nobel Laureate. In 1992 Eugene Fama and Kenneth French from the University of Chicago, Dartmouth College respectively, introduced their Multifactor Asset Pricing Model and Value Effect. Their research improved on the Sharpe's single-factor asset-pricing model (CAPM). It identified market, size and value factors in returns. Their development of the three-factor asset-pricing model is an invaluable asset allocation and portfolio analysis tool, and revolutionizes the way investors and advisors construct and analyze portfolios. Nobel Laureate, Paul Samuelson, determined that market prices are the best estimates of value, price changes follow random patterns, and future stock prices are unpredictable. Fama's Efficient Market Theory further stated that it should be impossible to outperform the overall market through expert stock selection or market timing, and that the only way an investor can possibly obtain higher returns is by purchasing riskier investments.

We also have the introduction of the "Efficient Frontier." The Efficient Frontier gives the best return that can be expected for a given level of risk or the lowest level of risk needed to achieve a given expected rate of return. Typically, the portfolios that comprise the Efficient Frontier are the ones that are most highly diversified. Less diversified portfolios tend to be closer to the middle of the achievable region. Putting this all together we learned from The Financial Analysis Journal May/June 1991 and subsequent studies that the proper allocation of those diverse funds was a 91.5% determinant of portfolio performance. Stock selection, market timing and other factors in total account for only about 8.5%

In the Journal of Finance, December 1965, A. G. Becker Corp. introduced their "Green Book" performance tables comparing results to benchmarks. These are the first studies showing that investment professionals fail to outperform market indexes. In 1977 Roger Ibbotson and Rex Sinquefield did extensive database studies of securities prices, collecting extensive public market information dating back to 1926. Based upon strong simplifying assumptions, Capital Asset Pricing Model (CAPM) concludes that the market portfolio sits on the efficient frontier. Finally with John McQuown and Rex Sinquefield came the birth of the index fund. Now we could take advantage of purchasing the entire market.

Summary:
- Diversify between the major asset and sub-asset categories.
- Properly allocate between the major asset and sub-asset categories.
- Use low cost index or asset allocated funds.
- Use the Multifactor Asset Pricing Model (MAPM) and the Capital Asset Pricing Model (CAPM), to recognize market, size and value factors in building your "Efficient Frontier."

In the real world, it is very difficult to find two or three mutually uncorrelated asset classes and pretty much impossible to find four. Fortunately, we do not need four completely uncorrelated to get the benefits of diversification. Some historically weakly correlated asset classes you might want for your portfolio are US large-cap stocks, US small-cap value stocks, foreign large-cap stocks, foreign small-cap stocks, short-term US bonds, short-term foreign bonds, real estate, and possibly some commodities.

Now let us build a portfolio and see how we can achieve a high amount of return with a lower exposure to risk. This is a generalized example, not a rendering of personalized

Investment Success

investment advice or service. Your actual portfolio needs to be specifically personalized to fit your individual circumstance.

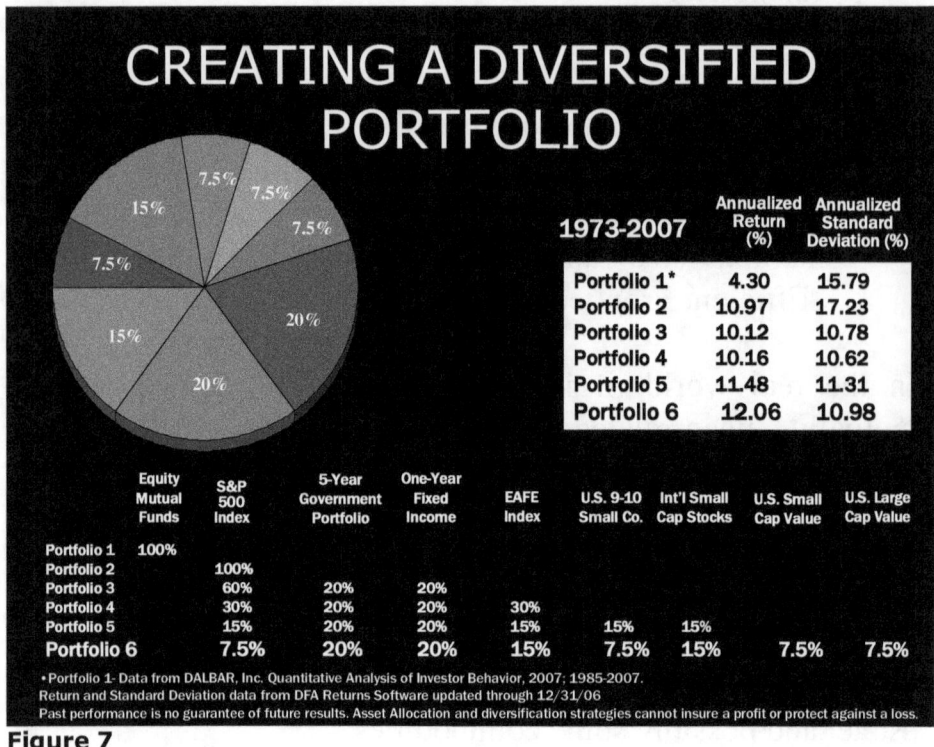

CREATING A DIVERSIFIED PORTFOLIO

1973-2007	Annualized Return (%)	Annualized Standard Deviation (%)
Portfolio 1*	4.30	15.79
Portfolio 2	10.97	17.23
Portfolio 3	10.12	10.78
Portfolio 4	10.16	10.62
Portfolio 5	11.48	11.31
Portfolio 6	12.06	10.98

	Equity Mutual Funds	S&P 500 Index	5-Year Government Portfolio	One-Year Fixed Income	EAFE Index	U.S. 9-10 Small Co.	Int'l Small Cap Stocks	U.S. Small Cap Value	U.S. Large Cap Value
Portfolio 1	100%								
Portfolio 2		100%							
Portfolio 3		60%	20%	20%					
Portfolio 4		30%	20%	20%	30%				
Portfolio 5		15%	20%	20%	15%	15%	15%		
Portfolio 6		7.5%	20%	20%	15%	7.5%	15%	7.5%	7.5%

•Portfolio 1- Data from DALBAR, Inc. Quantitative Analysis of Investor Behavior, 2007; 1985-2007.
Return and Standard Deviation data from DFA Returns Software updated through 12/31/06
Past performance is no guarantee of future results. Asset Allocation and diversification strategies cannot insure a profit or protect against a loss.

Figure 7

Portfolio One looks at the timeframe from 1985-2006. Based on the study done by the Dalbar group, which measured actual investor behavior; we see drastically different results from the published return of the mutual funds as a whole. The annualized rate of return for investors investing in equity-based mutual funds, from 1985-2006, was a dismal 4.3%. The annualized deviation for this portfolio was 15.97%.

Our second portfolio compares what the results would have been had the investor simply stayed with a 100% Standard & Poors Index stock portfolio, using DFA Software 1973 through 2007 to determine the results. The annualized return in this portfolio increased to 10.97% but the standard deviation also increased, to 17.23%.

In Portfolio Three we have begun the diversification process. We allocate only 60% to stocks and the remaining 40% to fixed assets, using 20% in a 5-year government bond portfolio and 20% in 1-year fixed income. The results are a slight decrease in returns to 10.12%, but a substantial decrease in standard deviation to only 10.78%.

In Portfolio Four we keep the same 60% stock / 40% fixed ratio, but we split the stock portion in half. We keep 50% of the stock portfolio in the S&P 500 and allocate the remaining 50% to International Large Cap stocks using the MSCI EAFE Index. MSCI EAFE stands for Morgan Stanley Capital International; the EAFE acronym stands for Europe, Australasia, and Far East. In this portfolio we begin to again raise the performance results, to 10.16% and lower the standard deviation to 10.62%.

We now have 40% fixed and 60% in stock, divided 1/2 of the total in Larger Cap US stocks and 1/2 of the total in International Large Cap stocks. In Portfolio Five we introduce the "size" factor by splitting the 30% that we have in each the US Large Cap and the International Large Cap. This will leave 15% in United States Large Cap and 15% in International Large Cap and add 15% United States Small Cap and International Small Cap. These results would have increased the annualized return over the 11% mark to 11.48%. It also increases the standard deviation to 11.31%.

Investment Success

In our last scenario Portfolio Six, we have introduced the "value" concept. We have split the remaining 15% in the United States Large Cap in half, putting the other 7.5% into US Large Cap Value. We also have reduced the US Small Cap in half to 7.5% and added 7.5% of US Mid Cap Value. This gives us our best performance balance. This last scenario gives us an annualized return of over 12% to 12.06%. It also gives us a standard deviation of only 10.98%.

This is how we go about building a portfolio using the principles offered through our scholars and Nobel Prize Laureates. We have taken into consideration diversification, correlation, cost, market, size, and value to build a portfolio that is well allocated for this hypothetical client.

Chapter 13
Financial Advisors; Who needs 'em?

After explaining to you that **Allocation, Allocation and Allocation** are the three most important things in determining the success of your portfolio, you might wonder why you would ever want to employ a Financial Advisor. Fair enough.

To some degree, this depends on your unique situation, but most will find that they are better off seeking the information, expertise, experience, and discipline provided by a financial advisor. I have said earlier that investing was simple but not easy. The question is, do you need professional help in order to design and stick to an effective financial plan? In my experience it is extremely difficult to first be truthful with yourself in making this design. Once the plan is designed it seems to be even more difficult to stick with that plan when turbulence takes over the financial markets. You should not change your allocation because the market has changed. You should change your allocation when something in your living situation has changed.

How do you go about determining the proper allocation for you?

- Age – A person who has 30 working years ahead of him may be able to sustain more volatility than one just entering retirement
- Life Expectancy – How long does your money need to last?
- Life Values – Simple life or travel and eat at the best restaurants.

- Spending needs – Medical, college for kids or grandkids.
- Attitude toward inheritance – Leave all to kids or die penniless.
- Attitude toward gifting – Church, friends, other charities.
- Risk tolerance – You need to be able to sleep at night.

Professional financial help goes far beyond picking stocks. If your advisor's only value proposition is stock or fund picking, then there may indeed be a case to be made for firing him or her. If your advisor isn't required by law to serve the client's best interests, you may want to replace him or her. If you and your advisor have a built in conflict of interests you might want to fire him or her.

Hiring an advisor, however, arms you with expertise and resources with which to approach planning your financial future. This coaching and support can help you to smoothly endure and make the most of the circumstances in your life such as career, marriage, children, assets, liabilities, etc. Furthermore, a financial professional provides the emotional discipline required to make sure plans are acted upon. He or she provides guidance, reassurance, support and stability to help you stay on course and reach your long-term goals. Using myself as an example, I find it more difficult to manage my own portfolio than I do others. When I manage my own, I fall into the same traps as I have described, being honest with myself in choosing an allocation and sticking with it in good times and in bad.

In my admittedly biased opinion, the do-it-yourself (DIY) option would be penny wise and pound-foolish. Do advisors add enough value to justify their fees? Just remember that many elements of financial advice never show up on a quarterly portfolio report. And it is difficult with the upfront charges, annual charges, and costs of buying and selling along with the other charges not easily recognized, to determine the total costs for your investment. An article in the Wall Street Journal Sunday, on May 22, 2005 took a stab at it. They said that Wall Street is devouring 2% of your portfolio value each year if you are a do-it-yourself investor and maybe 3% if you use an investment advisor.

Costs of Wall Street

...they are devouring

2% of your portfolio value each year if you are a do-it-yourself investor.

3% if you use an investment advisor.

Source: Wall Street Journal Sunday, ABJ May 22, 2005

Figure 8

Investment Success

Making quality financial decisions requires an ample commitment to learning and research. While the Internet's easy access to information has helped to make it feasible for individuals to independently manage their finances, the magnitude of investment skills and information that you need can be overwhelming. The financial world is filled with foreign concepts, esoteric language, legal rules, and difficult methodologies. Whether you want to develop a portfolio, plan for retirement, pay for college, or reach any other major financial goal, there are professionals who have spent their careers serving people with the same concern, and it is a good idea to take advantage of their experience.

An investment in financial management provides peace of mind by ensuring your best odds of permanent wealth and comfort. This planned approach to success is the result of a multi-step process. You must:

- Set achievable financial and personal goals.
- Assess your current financial health by examining your assets, liabilities, income, insurance, taxes, investments and estate plan.
- Develop a realistic, comprehensive plan to meet your financial goals by addressing financial weaknesses and building on financial strengths.
- Put your plan into action and monitor its progress.
- Revise your plan to accommodate changing goals, changing personal circumstances, changing financial opportunities, and changing market and tax laws.

The planning process requires skill, knowledge, diligence, and discipline, but great reward makes it well worth the time and effort. Even if you feel competent enough to develop a plan of your own, a financial advisor can act as a sounding board for your ideas and help you focus on your goals, using his or her broad knowledge of areas such as estate planning and investments. Sometimes we need the help of others. This is a fact of life, and one that also applies to our financial decisions. That is why many will seek the services of a financial advisor. Whether we lack the time to do a lot of research ourselves or we feel the need for a professional opinion, financial advisors can be convenient and helpful. It often helps to be joined in life's journey by a financial advisor — someone who knows the latest financial rules and can advise us today and help us with our future financial needs.

In today's world, proper financial planning is more important than ever! With increasingly complex financial markets, longer life expectancies and uncertainty about Social Security and long-term health care coverage, choosing the right investments could play a critical role in helping to secure your financial future. With more than 10,000 different investments and funds to choose from, one of the most important decisions you can make about your future is to seek the advice of a qualified investment professional.

No financial advisor gives foolproof advice. As everyone knows, financial markets are fickle and can turn on a dime. However, a good financial advisor will try to minimize the financial risks for you by gaining an understanding of your particular situation and lifestyle goals. The financial advisor must be aware of all of your assets, your current lifestyle, and your retirement goals.

Almost everyone has an opinion on the value of financial advice and the extent to which it is needed. But since good advice often involves discipline, process, perspective and similar things that are not easily quantified, there's no consensus on the profile of a person who should use an advisor as opposed to one who might be successful going it alone. In general, it seems most consumers want to work with a qualified advisor who understands and responds to their needs and circumstances. For them, it is often important to talk to someone face to face, and regular contact is also important. These people often feel overwhelmed and look to a reliable third party to organize affairs and simplify decision-making.

For instance, a landmark study conducted by CEG Worldwide examined investor behavior for the period from January 1990 to March 2000. Aptly entitled *Investors Behaving Badly*, it showed quite compellingly that most advisors have a positive impact on their clients' financial lives. It also showed that the traditional foundations of financial planning, such as setting financial goals, were often not in place for do-it-yourself investors (DIY), who were more inclined to be moved by short-term influences as a result. All else being equal, do-it-yourself investors were shown to be more likely to trade too frequently, which more often than not led to poor market timing. It is well documented that portfolio turnover correlates negatively to returns. These do-it-yourself investors often chase a hot stock, hot fund or hot asset class, effectively buying near the top of the market when they do so. As a result, the study found that many DIY investors missed out on potentially better results through failed attempts at market timing. Investors are supposed to buy low and sell high, but it seems that most are naturally inclined to buy high. In 1996, 5.5 years was the average holding period for mutual funds. By 2000, with markets on a veritable tear, the typical long-term holding period had dropped to 2.9 years. Today, it is less than one year on average. How's that for discipline and a long-term perspective?

At any rate, most people know intuitively whether they want to work with an advisor. Ultimately, it is a decision about value, where cost is one half of the story and benefit is the other. Everyone needs to recognize that different people define value in different ways. Speaking personally, I've never found a way to put a meaningful price on "constructive behavior modification." Personally, I believe that people should, at a minimum, possess the "Three Ts" necessary to manage their own financial affairs: time, temperament and training.

Here's a quick self-diagnostic exercise to help you determine which group you fall into:
Time
- Do you review your portfolio at least annually, even if you change nothing?
- Do you act without being reminded of major deadlines?
- Do you plan for your future in a meaningful way?
- Are you a "doer" who is not inclined to procrastinate?
Temperament
- Do you maintain your asset allocation in turbulent markets?
- Do you maintain your savings rate over time?

- Do you sleep as well as usual in turbulent markets?

Training

- Do you have the capacity to handle your own circumstances?
- Are you even aware of how complex your situation is?
- Are you aware of planning concepts beyond basic strategies?

If you honestly answered yes to all 10 questions, you probably do not need an advisor. If you answered no only once or twice, you might need one. If you answered no three or more times, you likely should be working with an advisor. I know there are people who can honestly answer yes to all 10 questions. Most people, I suspect, cannot.

Let us talk about the do-it-yourself investor

- Cost is about 2% of your portfolio value annually.
- Do you have the time?
- Do you have the discipline?
- Can you be truthful with yourself?
- Do you have the desire?

Professional Advisor

- Costs about an additional 1% of your portfolio value annually.
- Has the schooling experience and credentials.
- Their day is devoted to keeping up on trends.
- Can provide an objective opinion.
- May have access to investments that are out of reach to you.

I suggest that you choose an advisor who not only understands the markets but also, and most importantly, will take the time to understand you. Most people wouldn't think twice about hiring an attorney or finding a good medical doctor. A good financial advisor should fit into this same category. Ethics are table stakes in choosing a Financial Advisor. Does your advisor provide services with honesty and trust. Are his or her interests your interests, or the interests of the company they work for? Does he or she have the education, registration and certification required to properly represent you?

You might also ask yourself if you would feel more comfortable with a young energetic person starting his practice right out of school or with an elder statesman who has lived through the 60s, had first hand experience with economic ups and downs, marriage, children, grandchildren and the sickness and death of friends and relatives. Ask how the advisor gets paid. Is he or she commission based or fee based? Under the commission system, a broker is compensated on the basis of the number and size of transactions executed. With a fee-based account, compensation is based on the value of the account. Fee-based accounts are performance-driven, not commission-driven. Ask yourself if you feel that an advisor who is paid commissions with each transaction can be as client focused as one who receives his compensation based on the value of your account.

You might also want to know how many clients your prospective Financial Advisor serves. Can an advisor with 2,000 accounts afford you the same attention as one with 200? Finally give your perspective Financial Advisor a "gut" check or as I like to call it the "Bob Dillon test." "Does it feel right?" The value of the gut test should not be overlooked. Does the advisor seem to be client-centered? Does he or she appear interested in whether they can serve you efficiently and effectively? Does the advisor seem to be overly anxious to sell you as a client rather than express a desire to determine if the two of you will be a good "fit?" Can you work with this person?

The Mass Affluent Do you feel rich? Who serves your financial interests? There are only 430,000 really, truly, indisputably, wealthy households; those endowed with more than $10 million in investable wealth. So says *Financial Planning*, July 2005. I am not one of them. There is also a class called called the "Mass Affluent." I fit here, but I do not feel very affluent at all. The mass affluent market includes individuals and small business owners with between $100,000 and $1 million in investable assets. Simply stated, mass affluents are the market below the affluent market and above the mass market according to AIG, Rev 12/2004.

This market encompasses not only myself but most of my client base. Most of us do not feel very rich. In fact, many of us feel that we are just making it. Who services this market's financial needs?

Financial Planning in July 2005 stated that Paine Webber [now UBS Financial Services] didn't mind that its business with the mass affluent declined from nearly two-thirds of the total in 1994 to 51% in 2004. And so it was at the big brokerage houses as they to sought society's big winners. This development would be unremarkable except for the irony that the big brokerages, notably Merrill Lynch, had pioneered the so-called "democratization of wealth management" that virtually invented the mass affluent. Now like a nanny lured away by a richer family, these great caregivers of household wealth seem to have abandoned the little people they brought up in the world.

But the effect, of course, has been to breed a new host of financial caregivers, from monstrous banks to solo practitioners, ready to take the brokerages place at the sides of 20 million households unattended by the likes of Merrill. *On Wall Street, March*, 2004 states "investors with between $100,000 and $1 million in investable assets want more advice than most online discounters provide but, for whatever reason, do not want to use a traditional brokerage firm."

According to the Corporate Executive Board of the Financial Services Industry Council, institutions try to save on costs by serving the mass affluent via standard mass market service offerings and scaled delivery platforms. Not finding appropriate value propositions at their mass market focused initiatives, the mass affluent go elsewhere, in particular to independent financial planners.

Wall Street & Technology, 2002 says [Mass Affluent] investors have lost confidence in their ability to manage and expand their own wealth and they are increasingly turning to human advisors for professional guidance. Sapiens Tech, 2004 adds that self-investors, after a period of hype, have come to a realization: the vast amounts of readily available financial information, does not necessarily translate into sound investment decisions.

Who needs the assistance of a Financial Advisor? Probably you!

Get pointed in the right direction!

Investment Success

A few final thoughts:

- Learn this from me or let the market teach you. The only thing is that the market charges a high tuition.
- With capitalism you get a positive return on capital.
- Selling at the bottom and buying at the top are natural for most people.
- Time in the Market is more important than Market Timing
- I do not have people with investment problems; I have investments with people problems.
- Even though allocation accounts for 92% of success, many investors and advisors want to concentrate on the other 8%.
- Do not just chase returns!
- Relax!!!!

Glossary

12b-1 fees get their name from a section in the Investment Company Act of 1940. Today they are mainly used to reward intermediaries for selling a fund's shares. A 12b-1 fee is one that is charged by some mutual funds (usually actively managed funds), which is used to pay marketing, distribution, and service costs, and is paid to the broker. The Financial Industry Regulation Authority (FINRA) allows funds to charge as much as 1.00% annually as a 12b-1 fee.

A Random Walk Down Wall Street is an influential book written by Burton Malkiel, a Princeton economist, on the subject of stock markets. Malkiel argues that asset prices typically exhibit signs of random walk and that one can not consistently outperform market averages.

"A" Shares of Mutual Funds charge a front-end load at the time of purchase. This is a sales fee that is charged as a percentage of the total investment and is used to compensate the financial representative who sells the fund. The amount of the front-end load is subtracted from the original investment.

A. G. Becker Corporation started the financial consulting industry with the creation of their "Green Book" performance tables comparing results to benchmarks.

Accredited Asset Management Specialist (AAMS) designees have a broad knowledge of asset management. They seek to identify, analyze, and recommend strategies that are appropriate for client needs.

Alzheimer's Association is the only national non-profit organization dedicated to conquering Alzheimer's disease through research, and to providing education and support to people with the disease, their families and caregivers.

Alzheimer's Disease is a brain disorder named for German physician Alois Alzheimer, who first described it in 1906. It is a progressive and fatal brain disease. Alzheimer's destroys brain cells, causing problems with memory, thinking and behavior severe enough to affect work, lifelong hobbies or social life. As many as 5.3 million Americans are living with Alzheimer's disease today.

Annuities are contracts between you and an insurance company, under which you make a lump-sum payment or series of payments. In return, the insurer agrees to make periodic payments to you beginning immediately or at some future date.

Asset Allocation is the process of selecting the correct mixture of asset classes for your individual circumstance.

Asset Allocation Funds are Mutual Funds that vary the proportion of its portfolio devoted to stocks, bonds, and money market securities in order to reduce the variability of returns and to take better advantage of different segments of the securities markets. An asset allocation fund is designed to save individual investors from being required to alter their investment mix in response to changes in market conditions

Asset Class is a specific category of assets or investments, such as stocks, bonds, and cash. Assets within the same class generally exhibit similar characteristics, behave similarly in the marketplace, and are subject to the same laws and regulations.

"B" Shares of Mutual Funds charge back-end loads. When an investor purchases the B shares of a mutual fund, the sales charge is deferred until the fund is sold. This deferred load usually decreases each year. B shares typically charge a higher asset-based sales charge than Class A shares.

Banz, Rolf a 1981 University of Chicago Ph.D., published *"The Relationship between Return and Market Value of Common Stocks"* in the *Journal of Financial Economics*. The conclusion was startling: Between 1931 and 1974, small-company stocks had thrashed the market's giants. This new evidence dovetailed beautifully with Modern Portfolio Theory. MPT argued that risk was linked with return. Since small-cap stocks unquestionably carried higher risks than large-cap stocks, it would only be logical for them to deliver higher returns.

Bear Market is a market condition in which the prices of securities are falling, and widespread pessimism causes the negative sentiment to be self-sustaining. Bear markets rarely provide great entry points, as timing the bottom is very difficult to do.

Bull Market is a market condition in which prices are rising or are expected to rise. They are characterized by optimism, investor confidence and expectations that strong results will continue. It's difficult to predict consistently when the trends in the market will change.

"C" Shares of Mutual Funds typically do not impose a front-end load, but will often charge a nominal fee if the shares are sold within one year. Class C shares often impose a high asset-based sales charge.

Capital Asset Pricing Model (CAPM) was originally developed in 1952 by Harry Markowitz and fine-tuned over a decade later by others, including Nobel Laureate, William Sharpe. The model describes the relationship between risk and expected return, and it serves as a model for the pricing of risky securities.

Capital Structure Irrelevance Principle of Franco Modigliani and Merton Miller forms the basis for modern thinking on capital structure. The basic theorem states that the value of a firm is unaffected by how that firm is financed. It does not matter if the firm's capital is raised by issuing stock or selling debt. It also does not matter what the firm's dividend policy is. Capital Structure Irrelevance Principle is also called the Modigliani-Miller theorem (MM). Modigliani was awarded the 1985 Nobel Prize in Economics for this and other contributions. Miller was awarded the 1990 Nobel Prize in Economics.

CEG Worldwide provides coaching, consulting and research services for top-tier financial advisors and the institutions that serve them.

Center for Research in Security Prices (CRSP) is a part of the University of Chicago Booth School of Business, dedicated to providing the most complete, accurate, and easily usable securities data to all of its users. Six of the Chicago Booth faculty members have won Nobel Prizes.

Certified Financial Planner (CFP®) The College for Financial Planning was originally founded to formalize financial planning, set high standards, and establish a rigorous certification process for financial services professionals. In 1972, the College for Financial Planning introduced the Certified Financial Planner™ certification. CFP® certification has evolved into the world's most recognized and respected financial planning credential, with more than 50,000 professionals in the United States having earned the designation.

Certified Senior Advisor (CSA)® is an accreditation bestowed by the Society of Senior Advisors (SCSA®) on those who have supplemented their individual professional licenses, credentials and education with knowledge about aging and working with seniors. The SCSA® educates professionals to work more effectively with their senior clients. They believe that the right kind of planning, recommendations and referrals can make aging a state to be savored instead of a fate to be feared. For those who work with seniors, that means understanding the key health, social and financial factors that are important to seniors and how these factors work together.

Charles W. Myers Investment Group is an Independent Financial Consulting firm headed by Charles W. Myers CSA®. Charles W. Myers CSA® is an Investment Advisor Representative (IAR) registered under the Registered Investment Advisor (RIA) firm, True Wealth Management. They specialize in providing financial coaching to individual investors at all levels. Their goal is to help you live the one life you have in the best way you can without undue financial sacrifice or overexposure to risk.

Correlation is a statistical measurement of the relationship between two variables. In investing it measures how much you can expect different securities or asset classes to change in price relative to each other.

DALBAR, INC. develops standards for, and provides research, ratings, and rankings of intangible factors to the mutual fund, broker/dealer, discount brokerage, life insurance, and banking industries. This includes investor behavior, customer satisfaction, service quality, communications, Internet services, and financial-professional ratings.

Depression is an economic term not specifically defined. The simple definition is a recession that lasts longer and has a larger decline in business activity. Some would define a Depression as any economic downturn where real Gross Domestic Product (GDP) declines by more than 10 percent.

Dimensional Fund Advisors (DFA), is an innovative, world renouned, investment firm headquartered in Austin, Texas. The company was founded in 1981 by David G. Booth and Rex Sinquefield, both M.B.A. graduates of the University of Chicago Booth School of Business. DFA's objective is to use the insights of Modern Portfolio Theory to produce more efficient investment vehicles. The company's board of directors includes Myron Scholes and Robert C. Merton, both of whom won the Nobel Prize for economics. The late Merton Miller, another Nobel Laureate, was also on the board of directors. The company rejects stock-picking and market timing and use enhanced indexing to design portfolios and limit trading costs. Dimensional has more than $160 billion under management as of 2007. Its hundreds of mutual funds, trusts, and other portfolios are offered only to institutional investors and to individuals through registered fee-based only investment advisers.

Durable Power of Attorney (POA) or letter of attorney in common law systems or mandate in civil law systems is an authorization to act on someone else's behalf in a legal or business matter.

Efficient Frontier is a set of portfolios that each maximizes expected return for a given level of risk. For every level of return, there is one portfolio that offers the lowest possible risk, and for every level of risk, there is a portfolio that offers the highest return. These combinations can be plotted on a graph. This meeting point of each level of risk and reward, where the optimal portfolios reside, is called the "Efficient Frontier." Typically, the portfolios that comprise the Efficient Frontier are the ones that are most highly diversified. Less diversified portfolios tend to be closer to the middle of the achievable region.

Efficient Market Theory evolved in the 1960s from the Ph.D. dissertation of Eugene Fama who made the argument that in an active market that includes many well-informed and intelligent investors, securities will be appropriately priced and reflect all available information. If a market is efficient, no information or analysis can be expected to result in outperformance of an appropriate benchmark.

Exchange Traded Funds (ETF) are mutual funds that track an index, but can be traded like a stock. ETFs always bundle together the securities that are in an index; they never track actively managed mutual fund portfolios. Because ETFs are traded on stock exchanges, they can be bought and sold at any time during the day (unlike most mutual funds). Their price will fluctuate from moment to moment, just like any other stock's price. ETFs are more tax-efficient than normal mutual funds, and since they track indexes they have very low operating and transaction costs associated with them. There are no sales loads or investment minimums required to purchase an ETF.

Equity Indexed Annuity (EIA) is a special type of hybrid annuity. During the accumulation period, when you make either a lump sum payment or a series of payments, the insurance company credits you with a return that is based on changes in an equity index, such as the S&P 500 Composite Stock Price Index.

Fama, Eugene F. is widely recognized as the "father of modern finance." Fama's financial research is well known in both the economics and investment community. He is strongly identified with research on markets, particularly with regard to the efficient market hypothesis. Through his research he has brought an empirical and scientific rigor to the field of investment management, transforming the way finance is viewed and conducted. In 1992 he along with Kenneth French, introduced their Multifactor Asset Pricing Model and Value Effect. Their research improved on the Sharpe's single-factor asset-pricing model (CAPM). It identified market, size and value factors in returns. Their development of the three-factor asset-pricing model is an invaluable asset allocation and portfolio analysis tool, and revolutionizes the way investors and advisors construct and analyze portfolios. Fama is also chairman of the Center for Research in Security Prices at Chicago Booth. He is director of research at Dimensional Fund Advisors (DFA).

Fiduciary is a legal relationship of confidence or trust between two or more parties. Latin meaning "trust." It refers to a business or person who may act for another with total trust, good faith, and honesty who has the complete confidence and trust of that person. This means the adviser must hold the client's interest above his own in all matters. Conflicts of interest should be avoided at all costs. A Registered Investment Advisor (RIA) has a fiduciary responsibility to his/her client. A Registered Representative (RR) does not.

Financial Advisor (Adviser) is a generic term or job title, and may be used by investment professionals who may not hold any specific designation.

Financial Industry Regulation Authority (FINRA) is the largest non-governmental regulator for all securities firms doing business in the United States. FINRA is now performing the duties formerly performed by the National Association of Securities Dealers (NASD).

Fixed Annuities (FA) are contracts sold by an insurance company guaranteed that you will earn a minimum rate of interest during the time that your account is growing. The insurance company also guarantees that the periodic payments will be a guaranteed amount per dollar in your account.

French, Kenneth, is the Carl E. and Catherine M. Heidt Professor of Finance at the Tuck School of Business, Dartmouth College. He is President Elect of the American Finance Association. French is a director at Dimensional Fund Advisors in Austin, Texas where he also works as Consultant and Head of Investment Policy. In 1992 he along with Eugene Fama, introduced their Multifactor Asset Pricing Model and Value Effect. Their research improved on the Sharpe's single-factor asset-pricing model (CAPM). It identified market, size and value factors in returns. Their development of the three-factor asset-pricing model is an invaluable asset allocation and portfolio analysis tool, and revolutionizes the way investors and advisors construct and analyze portfolios.

Growth Funds are equity stock fund that invests in fastest growing firms, typically growing at an average rate of 10 percent per year, with capital appreciation as its primary objective. Such funds take more risk and pay a premium for stocks with above average earnings. When a stock market declines, a growth fund's earnings decline faster than the overall rate, and when the stock market rallies its earnings grow faster the overall rate.

Health Care Power of Attorney authorizes another person to act in our behalf in financial matters. It is effective when signed and continues to be effective even if the principle becomes incapacitated or incompetent.

Ibbotson, Roger is a professor of finance at Yale School of Management and is an expert on capital market returns, cost of capital, and international investment. He is the former chairman and founder of Ibbotson Associates, a financial research and information firm that was acquired by Morningstar, Inc. in 2006. His book with Rex A. Sinquefield, Stocks, Bonds, Bills and Inflation, updated in annual yearbooks, serves as the standard reference for information on investment market returns. Professor Ibbotson received a Ph.D. from the University of Chicago, an MBA from Indiana University, and a B.S. from Purdue University.

Index Fund is a passively managed mutual fund that tries to mirror the performance of a specific index, such as the S&P 500. Since portfolio decisions are automatic and transactions are infrequent, expenses tend to be lower than those of actively managed funds.

Inflation is the overall general upward price movement of goods and services in an economy, usually as measured by the Consumer Price Index

Investment Time Horizon is the period of time an investor expects to be able to grow a portfolio before needing the money.

Large Cap Stocks are shares of larger-sized companies, which are generally considered to be companies whose total outstanding shares are valued at $10 billion or more.

Lend it money is the money that you lend to an entity for a term longer than a year. This asset class would include bonds, which are loans to a large entity such as a corporation, municipality or the U.S. Government.

Living Will is a legal document that allows you to expresses your desires regarding the use of life-sustaining procedures on yourself.

Malkiel, Burton is an American economist and writer, most famous for his classic finance book A Random Walk Down Wall Street. He is a leading proponent of the efficient market hypothesis, which contends that prices of publicly traded assets reflect all publicly available information. He is a professor of economics at Princeton University, and is a two-time chairman of the economics department there. He served as a member of the Council of Economic Advisers (1975-1977), president of the American Finance Association (1978), and dean of the Yale School of Management (1981-1988).

Markowitz, Harry, a 1990 Nobel Prize winner in Economics, is currently a professor of finance at the Rady School of Management at the University of California, San Diego (UCSD). He is best known for his pioneering work in Modern Portfolio Theory, studying the effects of asset risk, return, correlation and diversification on probable investment portfolio returns.

Mass Affluent is a market which includes individuals and small business owners with between $100,000 and $1 million in investable assets.

Miller, Merton (1923-2000), was a Boston born Harvard educated, economist and educator who received the Nobel

Prize in Economics in 1990 for his and Merton Miller's theorem relating to corporate finance and that a company's value is unrelated to its dividend policy. The basic theorem states that in an efficient market the value of a firm is unaffected by how that firm is financed. It doesn't matter if the firm's capital is raised by issuing stock or selling debt. The Modigliani-Miller theorem (MM) is also often called the Capital Structure Irrelevance Principle.

Mid Cap Stocks are shares of medium-sized companies, which are generally considered to be companies whose total outstanding shares are valued between $1 and $10 billion.

Modern Portfolio Theory (MPT) is one of the most important and influential economic theories dealing with finance and investment. MPT was developed by Harry Markowitz and published under the title "Portfolio Selection" in the 1952 *Journal of Finance*. This theory recommends that the risk of a particular stock should not be looked at on a standalone basis, but rather in relation to how that particular stock's price varies in relation to the variation in price of the market portfolio.

Modgliani, Franco (1918-2003) was the Italian-born American economist and educator who received the Nobel Prize in Economics in 1985 for his and Merton Miller's theorem relating to corporate finance and that a company's value is unrelated to its dividend policy.

Modigliani-Miller Theorem (MM) was introduced by Nobel Laureates Franco Modigliani and Merton Miller. It states that in an efficient market the value of a firm is unaffected by how that firm is financed. It doesn't matter if the firm's capital is raised by issuing stock or selling debt. The Modigliani-Miller theorem (MM) is also often called the Capital Structure Irrelevance Principle.

MSCI EAFE Index stands for Morgan Stanley Capital International; the EAFE acronym stands for Europe, Australasia, and Far East.

Morningstar® Principia® is one of the most widely used resources in the financial planning industry. With a powerful research database that includes mutual funds, stocks, variable annuities, exchange-traded funds, closed-end funds, and separate accounts, advisors can conduct advanced research and analysis, monitor portfolios, and propose investment strategies.

Mutual Fund is a company that brings together a group of people and invests their money in stocks, bonds, and other securities. Each investor owns shares, which represent a portion of the holdings of the fund. As of early 2008, the worldwide value of all mutual funds totaled more than $26 trillion.

NASD stood for the National Association of Securities Dealers. It merged with the NYSE Regulation, Inc. in 2007 to form the organization now known as the Financial Industry Regulatory Authority (FINRA).

Nobel Laureate is a winner of a Nobel Prize which was established in the 1895 will of Swedish chemist and inventor Alfred Nobel. The Nobel Prize has grown in importance over the years to become the most important prize in their various fields. The grant is currently 10 million SEK, slightly more than US$1.2 million.

Own it money is your piece of the rock. This is exemplified by ownership in the company itself in the form of stock. Buying stock allows you to own part of Coca Cola, Microsoft, Enron or other companies.

Portfolio is a collection of investments all owned by the same individual or organization. These investments often include stocks, which are investments in individual businesses; bonds, which are investments in debt that are designed to earn interest; and mutual funds, which are essentially pools of money from many investors that are invested by professionals or according to indices.

Recession is a period of general economic decline; specifically, a decline in Gross Domestic Product GDP for two or more consecutive quarters.

Registered Investment Advisor (RIA) is an investment advisor firm who registers with the Securities and Exchange Commission (SEC) or their state and agree to be regulated by SEC rules. Being registered is often interpreted as a sign that the advisor meets a higher standard. RIA's have a fiduciary responsibility to act in the best interest of their client. They typically charge on a fee only payment plan. They must possess a Series 65 or 66 License.

Registered Representative (RR) is a person who works for a brokerage company that is licensed by the Security and

---

Exchange Commission (SEC) and acts as an account executive for clients trading investment products such as stocks, bonds and mutual funds. RR's do not have a fiduciary responsibility to act in the best interest of their client. Instead they must provide a product that is "suitable" for their customer. They typically work on commission. They must possess a Series 7 and Series 63 License.

Risk is the uncertainty tied to any investment decision. Many times when a Financial Advisor talks about risk he or she is talking about volatility.

Risk tolerance is your ability and willingness to lose some or all of your original investment in exchange for greater potential returns.

Samuelson, Paul of MIT, won a Nobel Prize in Economics in 1970. He determined that market prices are the best estimates of value, price changes follow random patterns, and future stock prices are unpredictable. He is famous for saying "Investing should be dull, like watching paint dry or grass grow. If you want excitement, take $800 and go to Las Vegas. It is not easy to get rich in Las Vegas, at Churchill Downs, or at the local Merrill Lynch office." Samuelson is among the last generalists to be incredibly productive in a number of fields in economics. He has contributed fundamental insights in consumer theory and welfare economics, finance theory, capital theory, dynamics and general equilibrium, and macroeconomics.

Securities and Exchange Commission (SEC) is the primary federal regulatory agency for the securities industry, whose responsibility is to promote full disclosure and to protect investors against fraudulent and manipulative practices in the securities markets.

Sharpe, William F. is the STANCO 25 Professor of Finance, Emeritus at Stanford University's Graduate School of Business. Dr. Sharpe is past President of the American Finance Association. In 1990 he received the Nobel Prize in Economics. He originated the use of his Capital Asset Pricing Model (CAPM), created for risk-adjusted investment performance analysis. The CAPM is a model for pricing an individual security or a portfolio. The market reward-to-risk ratio is effectively the market risk premium. In layman's terms, we know how much return can be expected in a very safe United States Treasury Bill. By gauging the risk and return of other securities or portfolios against this base we develop a standard deviation.

Sinquefield, Rex is the co-founder and past co-chairman of Dimensional Fund Advisors Inc., a Registered Investment Advisor (RIA) with over $160 billion under management. In the 1970s, he co-authored a series of papers and books titled *Stocks, Bonds, Bills & Inflation*, with Roger Ibbotson. These works provided the first seminal data on the performance of the financial market in the United States. At American National Bank of Chicago, he pioneered many of the nation's first index funds.

Small Cap Stocks are shares of companies with a relatively small market capitalization. The definition of small cap can vary among brokerages, but generally it is a company with a market capitalization of between $300 million and $2 billion.

Society of Senior Advisors (SCSA®) is a national organization that educates professionals to work more effectively with their senior clients. Founded in 1997, SCSA teaches an integrated approach to the health, financial, and social aspects of aging, with its focus on people. Professionals who obtain the designation as Certified Senior Advisors (CSA's) are able to integrate this knowledge into their professional practices.

Spend it money is your cash and your investments that can be liquidated into cash in a short period of time, usually within a year. This asset class would include passbook savings, checking accounts, short-term CDs, Government T-Bills and the money stuffed under your mattress.

Standard and Poors 500 Index (S&P 500) is a basket of 500 stocks that are considered to be widely held. The S&P 500 index was created in 1957, although it has been extrapolated backwards to several decades earlier for performance comparison purposes. This index provides a broad snapshot of the overall U.S. equity market. The index selects its companies based upon their market size, liquidity, and sector. Most of the companies in the index are solid mid cap or large cap corporations. Most experts consider the S&P 500 one of the best benchmarks available to judge overall U.S. market performance.

Standard Deviation is a statistical measurement of how far a variable quantity, such as the price of a stock, moves above or below its average value. The wider the range, which means the greater the standard deviation, the riskier an investment is considered to be. The Sharpe Ratio attempts to quantify an investment's risk relative to its investment performance. The higher the ratio, the better the investment's performance after adjusting for its risk.

Style Drift is the divergence of a mutual fund from its stated investment style or objective. Style drift occurs as a result of intentional portfolio investing decisions by management, a change of the fund's management or, in the case of stocks, a company's growth.

Stockbroker, also called Registered Representative (RR) is a licensed agent who has to pass certain qualifying tests (Series 7 & 63) to be certified to offer securities investment advice to investors. He or she may (1) counsel what and when to buy, (2) counsel whether to hold or sell securities, (3) execute buy-sell orders on behalf of the investors, and (4) charge a percentage of the transaction amount as brokerage fee for the services rendered.

TD AMERITRADE is an online broker with over 6 million U.S. customers, and many more internationally, that has grown rapidly through acquisition, to become the 746th-largest US firm in 2008.

Three Ts of Investing is a quick self-diagnostic exercise to help you determine if you possess the characteristics to manage your own financial affairs.
Time
- Do you review your portfolio at least annually, even if you change nothing?
- Do you act without being reminded of major deadlines?

- Do you plan for your future in a meaningful way?
- Are you a "doer" who is not inclined to procrastinate?

Temperament
- Do you maintain your asset allocation in turbulent markets?
- Do you maintain your savings rate over time?
- Do you sleep as well as usual in turbulent markets?

Training
- Do you have the capacity to handle your own circumstances?
- Are you even aware of how complex your situation is?
- Are you aware of planning concepts beyond basic strategies?

True Wealth Design is a fee-only investment advisory and financial planning firm that assists individuals and businesses with financial planning, investment planning, and retirement planning needs. They are committed to understanding client's unique situation and objectively develop a comprehensive strategy that is in the client's best interest to help them attain their goals.

United States Treasury Bill (T-Bill) is a negotiable debt obligation issued by the U.S. government and backed by its full faith and credit, having a maturity of one year or less.

Value Funds are mutual funds that invest in the so-called 'overlooked gems' firms with undistinguished earnings record but great potential for growth, or at the bottom phase of a cyclic business with the hope that they will not remain overlooked for long. They are a mutual fund that invests in companies that it determines to be underpriced by fundamental measures. Assuming that a company's share price will not remain undervalued indefinitely, the fund looks to make money by buying before the expected upturn. Value funds tend to focus on safety rather than growth, and often choose investments providing dividends as well as capital appreciation. They invest in companies that have low P/E ratios, and stocks that have fallen out of favor with mainstream investors, either due to changing investor preferences, a poor quarterly earnings report, or hard times in a particular industry. Value stocks are often mature companies that have stopped growing and that use their earnings to pay dividends. Thus value funds produce current income (from the dividends) as well as long-term growth (from capital appreciation once the stocks become popular again). They tend to have more conservative and less volatile returns than growth funds.

Variable Annuities (VA) are contracts between you and an insurance company, under which you make a lump-sum payment or series of payments. In return, the insurer agrees to make periodic payments to you beginning immediately or at some future date. Variable annuities are securities regulated by the SEC. The issuer pays a periodic amount linked to the investment performance of an underlying portfolio. They are are notorious for the fees they charge and for the high rate of commission paid to the seller. The average annual expense on variable annuity subaccounts currently stands at 2.44% of assets.

Volatility refers to how easily a stock tends to rise and fall. A volatile stock would be one that sees very large swings in its stock price. Many times when a Financial Advisor speaks of risk, he/she is speaking of volatility.

Investment Success

Works Cited

Abundant Technologies Inc. 21 Sept. 2008

<https://www.abundantadvisor.com/Connection/login.aspx>.

"Alzheimer's Disease Fact Sheet." National Institute on Aging. 12 Jan.

2009

<http://www.nia.nih.gov/Alzheimers/Publications/adfact.htm>.

"Annuities." U.S. Securities and Exchange Commission (Home Page).

10 Jan. 2009 <http://www.sec.gov/cgi-bin/txt-srch-

sec?text=annuities&section=Investor+Information>.

Banz, Rolf. "Morningstar Investing Classroom." Small Cap Advantage.

18 Apr. 2009

<http://news.morningstar.com/classroom2/printlesson.asp?docId

=4527&CN=com>.

"Beginners' Guide to Asset Allocation, Diversification, and

Rebalancing." U.S. Securities and Exchange Commission (Home

Page). 10 Jan. 2009

<http://www.sec.gov/investor/pubs/assetallocation.htm>.

Investment Success

Brinson, Gary P., Brian D. Singer, and Gilbert L. Beebower.

"Determinants of Portfolio. Performance II: An Update."

Financial Analysts Journal (1991).

"Can you trust your financial adviser? - MSN Money." 18 Mar. 2009

<http://articles.moneycentral.msn.com/RetirementandWills/Creat

eaPlan/CanYouTrustYourFinancialAdviser.aspx>.

Dalbar. Dalbar - The Measurement of Success. 2009. 18 Apr. 2009

<http://www.dalbarinc.com/content/showpage.asp?page=200106

2100>.

Fama, Eugene F., and Kenneth R. French. "The Cross-Section of

Expected Stock Returns." Journal of Finance (1992).

Fama, Eugene F. "Behavior of Stock Market Prices." Journal of Business

(1965).

"History." Dimensional Fund Advisors: DFA Home. 18 Apr. 2009

<http://www.dfaus.com/philosophy/history/>.

Ibbotson,, Roger. Path to Investing Leading the Way to Financial

Knowledge. 7 Nov. 2008

<http://www.pathtoinvesting.org/experts/pdfs/allocate.pdf>.

Investment Success

"In Today's Hot Market, Better Keep Your Cool - February 1, 2007."

Business, financial, personal finance news - CNNMoney.com.

2007. 18 Apr. 2009

<http://money.cnn.com/magazines/moneymag/moneymag_archiv

e/2007/02/01/8398749/index.htm>.

"Index Funds vs. Actively-Managed Funds." Mutual Funds. 16 Mar.

2009

<http://mutualfunds.about.com/od/activevspassivefunds/a/indexv

sactive.htm>.

"Investors Behaving Badly." 18 Apr. 2009

<http://www.camagazine.com/1/0/0/9/6/index1.shtml>.

Jensen, Michael C. "Performance of Mutual Funds in the Period 1945-

1964." Journal of Finance (1965).

Malkiel, Burton G. A Random Walk Down Wall Street, Completely

Revised and Updated Edition. Boston: W. W. Norton &

Company, 2003.

Malkiel, Burton G. Returns form Investing in Equity Funds 1971-1991.

2nd ed. Vol. 50. Journal of Finance, 1995.

Malkiel, Burton. "Returns from Investing in Equity Funds 1971-1991."

Journal of Finance 50 (1995).

Markowitz, Harry. Journal of Finance/American Finance Association. 7

(1952): 77-91.

"The Mass Affluent." Financial Planning. July 2005. June 2007

<http://www.financial-planning.com/>.

"Modern portfolio theory -." Wikipedia, the free encyclopedia. 18 Apr.

2009 <http://en.wikipedia.org/wiki/Modern_portfolio_theory>.

Morningstar Principia. Winter 2009

<http://corporate.morningstar.com/US/asp/subject.aspx?xmlfile=

41.xml&ad=07Cat&gclid=CNTdxe2n8ZkCFSbxDAodvWn6QQ

>.

"Nobel Laureates - Index Funds Advisors, Inc." Index Funds | DFA

Funds 18 Apr. 2009

<http://www.ifa.com/12steps/Step2/step2page3.asp>.

"PERSONAL FINANCE - Retirement Planning - Comcast.net." Finance,

Stock Quotes and Personal Finance - Comcast.net. 18 Apr. 2009

<http://finance.comcast.net/personalfinance/view.html?x=retirem

ent/investing/wrongannuities>.

"Principia Investment Advisors, LLC Advisor vs Stockbroker." Financial

Planner. 14 Feb. 2009

<http://www.piadv.com/advisor_stockbroker.html>.

Quinn, Jane Bryant. Making the Most of Your Money. New York:

Simon & Schuster, 1997.

"Recession Resource Center." Economics at About.Com 10 Jan. 2009

<http://economics.about.com/cs/businesscycles/a/recession.htm?t

erms=business+cycles>.

"Reduction of Risk Over Time - ICMA-RC." ICMA-RC: Building

Retirement Security - ICMA-RC. 18 Apr. 2009

<http://www.icmarc.org/xp/rc/marketview/chart/2008/20080215r

eductionofriskovertime.html>.

"Registered Investment Advisor -." Wikipedia. 14 Feb. 2009

<http://en.wikipedia.org/wiki/Registered_Investment_Advisor>.

"Registered investment advisor." Registered Investment Advisor. 18

Apr. 2009 <http://www.registered-investment-

advisor.com/wealth-manager-registered-rep.html>.

"Registered Investment Advisor Vs Registered Rep (Broker).18 Apr.

2009 <http://ezinearticles.com/?Registered-Investment-Advisor-

Vs-Registered-Rep-(Broker)&id=1023500>.

"Sapiens-Tech :: Our Team." Sapiens-Tech :: modeling your future

success. 2004. 2009 <http://www.sapiens-

tech.com/Dev2Go.web?Anchor=206923&rnd=1>.

"Schwab's Personal Choice Targets Mass Affluent". (01-MAR-04) On

Wall Street." AccessMyLibrary - News, Research, and

Information that Libraries Trust. 1 Mar. 2004. June 2007

<http://www.accessmylibrary.com/coms2/summary_0286-

20498147_ITM>.

"Separately managed accounts expected to explode | Wall Street &

Technology." Find Articles at BNET 2002. May 2007

<http://findarticles.com/p/articles/mi_hb338/is_200203/ai_n2420

9940/>.

Sinquefield, Rex. "Principia Investment Advisors, LLC. 18 Apr. 2009

www.piadv.com/advisor_stockbroker.html>.

"Stock Broker or Investment Advisor - What's the Difference?"

Whitcomb & Hess. 14 Feb. 2009

<http://www.whitcomb.com/documents/InFormSpring2007.pdf>.

"The stock market: Is it a trailing or leading indicator." Common Cents.

18 Apr. 2009

<http://commoncentsdg.blogspot.com/2009/01/stock-market-is-

it-trailing-or-leading.html>.

"Stockbroker, Financial Advisor, Financial Planner: Know The

Difference?" Financial Fitness. 14 Feb. 2009

<http://financialfitness.blogspot.com/2008/04/stockbroker-

financial-advisor-financial.html>.

"TD AMERITRADE Survey Reveals Need for Clarity." The Free

Library. 2004. Apr. 2009

<thefreelibrary.com/TD+AMERITRADE+Survey+Reveals+Nee

d+for+Clarity>.

Tulett, Matthews & Associates Inc. - Investment Counsel. 18 Apr. 2009

<http://www.tma-

invest.com/files/investment_research/History_of_Portfolio_Theo

ry_and_Investment_Management_Breakthroughs.pdf>.

"Understanding Financial Advice." <u>TD AMERITRADE Institutional -</u>

<u>Home Page</u>. 14 Feb. 2009

<http://www.tdainstitutional.com/pdf/UnderstandingFinancialAd

vice.ppt>.

"Variable Annuities: What You Need To Know." <u>U.S. Securities and</u>

<u>Exchange Commission (Home Page)</u>. 10 Jan. 2009

<http://www.sec.gov/answers/annuity.htm>.

"Wall Street Charges." <u>Wall Street Journal Sunday-ABJ</u> [New York] 22

May 2005.

"What's Wrong With Variable Annuities at SmartMoney.com." <u>Online</u>

<u>Investing: Stocks, Personal Finance & Mutual Funds at</u>

<u>SmartMoney.com</u>. 30 Jan. 2008. 10 Jan. 2009

<http://www.smartmoney.com/personal-finance/retirement/whats-

wrong-with-variable-annuities-9512>.

www.ingramcontent.com/pod-product-compliance
Lightning Source LLC
Chambersburg PA
CBHW051542170526
45165CB00002B/847